Good Little Hearts V3: Nelly Rivers' Great Riches

Aunt Fanny

GOOD LITTLE HEARTS.

NELLY RIVERS' GREAT RICHES.

𝔄 𝔖𝔲𝔫𝔡𝔞𝔶 𝔖𝔱𝔬𝔯𝔶.

BY AUNT FANNY,

AUTHOR OF "NIGHTCAPS," "MITTENS," "PET BOOKS," "POP-GUNS," "WIFE'S STRATAGEM," ETC.

"I love God, and little children." — RICHTER.

VOLUME III.

NEW YORK:
PUBLISHED BY HURD AND HOUGHTON,
401 BROADWAY, COR. WALKER ST.
1864.

Entered according to Act of Congress, in the year 1864, by
FANNY BARROW,
in the Clerk's Office of the District Court of the United States for the
Southern District of New York.

RIVERSIDE, CAMBRIDGE:
STEREOTYPED AND PRINTED BY
H. O. HOUGHTON AND COMPANY.

THE PARSONAGE. *Page 32.*

THIS LITTLE SUNDAY BOOK

IS DEDICATED TO

LIZZIE, ALBERTA, HARRY, AND DEAR LITTLE BABY "DOT":

FOUR GOOD LITTLE HEARTS.

MOTTO FOR ALL GOOD LITTLE HEARTS.

" Do all the good you can,
    In all the ways you can,
    To all the people you can,
    In every place you can,
    At all the times you can,
    As long as ever you can. "

CONTENTS.

——◆——

ILLUSTRATIONS.

———◆———

GOOD LITTLE HEARTS.

——◆——

NELLY RIVERS' GREAT RICHES.

INTRODUCTION.

ONE Sunday evening the "Pop-gun" children had been singing hymns, as usual, with their parents. They were now sitting quite silent and still, when suddenly Fred, looking very earnestly up in his mother's face, said,—— "Mamma, I wish Aunt Fanny would write a Sunday-story; I do declare, I mean to ask her!"

"Oh, do, do, do!" cried all the rest, with such a racket that you could hardly believe they were the silent children of a moment before. "Tell her, a Sunday-story is very much wanted to keep us in order."

"We shall do something dreadful some Sunday or other, if no other, Sunday," said Peter,

" if she don't take us in hand; and we 'll promise not to go perfectly wild with joy, but put
on our most serious good-boy and good-girl
looks when it comes. We 'll even behave better than when we are fast asleep."

The rest laughed at this, and their papa said,
" That is a very rash promise, Peter; for old
Mrs. Snarling says you are a tolerably good
boy when you are asleep, but a great torment
at all other times.".

Peter was just on the point of exclaiming,
" Bother old Mrs. Snarling!" but he recol-
lected himself in time, and made a loud " hem "
instead; upon which Sophie quietly remarked, —

" You seem to have a remarkably large frog
in your throat, Peter."

" I was swallowing Mrs. Snarling," he. answered; at which they all tried not to laugh,
out of politeness to the old lady.

But some chuckles would come, and their
mother gravely advised them to sing one more
hymn, and then be off for *Bed*fordshire.

This is the hymn they sung. It is like a prayer. I want you all to learn at least to *say* it, my darling good little hearts : —

* " Hear my prayer, O Heavenly Father,
    Ere I lay me down to sleep ;
Bid thy angels pure and holy
    Round my bed Thy vigils keep.

" Great my sins, but, oh, Thy mercy
    Far outweighs them every one ;
Down before Thy cross I cast them,
    Trusting in Thy help alone.

" Keep me through this night of peril,
    Underneath its boundless shade ;
Take me to Thy rest, I pray thee,
    When my pilgrimage is made.

" None shall measure out Thy patience
    By the span of human thought ;
None shall bound the tender mercies
    Which Thy Holy Son has brought.

" Pardon all my past transgressions,
    Give me strength for days to come ;
Guide and guard me with Thy blessing,
    Till thy angels bid me home."

* From *Household Words.*

The next morning Fred spread a very large
sheet of letter-paper before him, and wrote this
important epistle : —

FRED'S LETTER.

"DEAR AUNT FANNY, —

" Those bird's-nest stories in the last ' Good
Little Hearts ' were bul— I mean splendid!
I almost wrote ' bully,' but mother can't bear
the expression, and she gives me ten cents
every week that I do not say it once. I suppose she means writing it too, so I 'm glad I
stopped in time.

" A very learned old gentleman came to see
father last week. In the evening he amused
us very much with what he called ' tricks in
language.' He wrote the letters of the word
' time,' and made what he called au ' anagram-
matic palindrome.' I 'm sure I have n't the least
idea what these awful hard terms mean, but he
twisted and turned ' time ' into four words
which can be read up and down, backwards

and forwards, in all kinds of fashions, and still make the same words, which is very curious. Here they are : —

TIME

ITEM

METI

EMIT

They are all Latin words except the English one, ' time.' ' Item ' means ' likewise '; ' meti,' ' to be measured'; and 'emit,' 'he buys.' There, Aunt Fanny! I think I 'm getting quite learned; don't you?

" He asked us to spell the fate of all earthly things in two letters. Can you? I could, — after I was told, — D. K. He said a young lady once asked what phonography was. He took out his pencil and wrote this, — ' U. R. A. B. U. T. L. N. !' (You are a beauty, Ellen.) That was phonography; ' at which she was highly delighted.'

" Then this funny, learned old gentleman told

us of a curious conversation of a backwoods-
man who did not like to waste words : —

"' Whose house ? '

"' Mog's.'

"' Of what built ? '

"' Logs.'

"' Any neighbors ? '

"' Frogs.'

"' What is the soil ? '

"' Bogs.'

"' How is the climate ? '

"' Fogs.'

"' What do you eat ? '

"' Hogs.'

"' How do you catch them ? '

"' Dogs.'

" And here is one more,—I think the best
of all : —

"' I came for the saw, sir,' said a little fellow.

"' What saucer ? '

" ' Why, the saw, sir, that you borrowed.'

" ' I borrowed no saucer.'

" ' Sure you did, sir ; borrowed our saw, sir.'

" ' Be off!   I never saw your saucer ! '   .

" ' But you did, sir ; there 's the saw, sir ;
now, sir.'

" ' Oh, you want the *saw* ! '

" I *must* tell you the compliment · the old
Quaker paid : —

" ' I wish thee and thy folks loved me and
my folks as well as me and my folks love thee
and thy folks. For sure there never was folks,
since folks was folks, that ever loved folks half
so well as me and my folks love thee and thy
folks.'

" Now, Aunt Fanny, have n't I amused you ?
and don't you want to do something very particularly kind for us ?   Of course you do, and
you are perfectly crazy to know what it is, —
so I will hurry and tell you.

" We do *so* want a story written expressly

for Sunday, — a Sunday-story. We think we are getting to be remarkably good children, owing to the excellent examples set us in all your books; but then, you, see if you were to write one which fitted Sunday *exactly*, we should become little wonders immediately; and this would delight all the cats in the house, for I am afraid we chase them Sundays the same as other days.

"You see, it is *so* hard to live without making a noise. There is a poor little boy they call Dan, who lives in a lane not far from us, with just the very crossest old grandmother you ever heard of. She makes him keep so quiet that it's perfectly awful. So we gave him a nice tin trumpet one day, and told him to go into the woods and have a good blow-out. Here he is, Aunt Fanny. I've drawn him for you sitting on a stump, with his little bare toes all turned in, and his cheeks all puffed out, having a real good time.

FRED, PETER, AND BOB RUNNING AWAY FROM THE CROSS OLD WOMAN. *Page* 16.

"But, oh dear! one day as we were peaceably walking down the lane, the cross old grandmother rushed out of her cottage in a perfect  fume of rage to beat us with her cane for giving Dan the trumpet.

"'Oh, you little varmints!' she cried, 'you want Dan to crack my ears! You gave him a tin trumpet on purpose! I'd rather hear twenty-seven cannons going off at once.'

"Did n't we have to run! I first, then Peter, then little Bob, and the old woman after us shaking her stick, and scolding worse than two cats on a fence. Poor old thing! I feel sorry for her too. I dare say she has the rheumatism dreadfully, and no wonder she 's cross.

"I think this is enough for one letter, — don't you? And you *will* write a Sunday-

story, darling Aunt Fanny, — won't you ? and
we promise to be more ' *lovinger* ' than ever.
Bob told me to write it so. Next week, I
shall go to old Mrs. Marble, the postmistress,
and ask her for a letter for your affectionate
nieces and nephews,

" SOPHIE, FRED, and LOU ;
" PETER, KITTY, and BOB."

This time all the children went together to
the post-office, and bounced in upon Mrs. Marble so suddenly that she nearly fell off her
chair behind the counter.

" Look here, young house-a-fire ! " she cried,
shaking her knitting-needle at Fred, — " I wish
I was a little man, a-living by myself, and all
the bread and cheese I got I 'd put upon the
shelf. I don't know whether I 'm standing
on my wig or my stockings when you come
in, you fluster me so, — and now you 've gone
and brought all the rest ! The Great Plague
of London is nothin' to you."

" Well, Mrs. Marble, you must make the best of it. We have come to buy all sorts of things including nothing, and when the battered old mail-bag comes in, we expect you to hand us a big letter from Aunt Fanny. If you don't, we shall all fall a-crying."

" Look here, I guess all the tears *you* shed will be crocodile tears."

" And if we laugh, we are laughing hyenas, I suppose," said Fred, showing his teeth and uttering a ferocious " he, he, he ! " which set the other children screaming with merriment.

" Yes," returned the old lady, twinkling her eyes about half a hundred times, trying to look solemn and majestic, and keep from laughing herself. But it would not do, and she burst out as hearty as the rest, though she had n't a tooth in her head, saying, " Look here, young alligator, if you 're such a bad boy now, making fun of your elders and betters, I don't know what you will be when your whiskers are grown."

"Oh, you see, all my badness is coming out now; not a grain of fun or mischief will be left in me when I grow up. I shall be so brimful of learning and sense, that everybody will cry out as I walk the streets, ' Look here, there goes the great Dr. Frederic Blank.'"

The old lady dived for her old shoe to throw at Fred when " look here " came out; but he jumped off the barrel, on which he had been sitting, and ran out of the door, and the shoe fell into a keg of pickled mackerels.

" Hallo ! " cried Peter, pulling it out, " your shoe will keep forever now, Mrs. Marble ; it 's pickled."

" Yes, and it had better be fried, too," said the old lady. " Look here, you just go and lay it on the hearth in the kitchen, by the cooking-stove ; when it 's dry, I 'll fire it at young Bouncer again ! "

Just then the distant rumble of the mail-stage was heard, and the children went rushing

out to meet it. The old rattling thing soon
came round the corner, bumping and thumping and flumping and jumping over the ruts
in the road, knocking the heads of the passen-
gers within against the top and sides, and making them look both angry and astonished every
minute, with their hats and bonnets every which
way.

Down tumbled the old mail-bag; in an instant all six children were dancing around it,
clamóring for the key; and the stage went clat-
tering off, the people looking out of its windows, laughing, in spite of the dreadful bumps
they were getting, at the crazy capers of the
young ones.

"Here it is!" exclaimed Sophie, as the old
lady fished a great yellow envelope out of the
bag. "Oh, how nice and thick! Here's our
Sunday-story, I'm sure!"

"Sunday-story? Look here, what does that
mean?" asked Mrs. Marble.

"We 'll read Aunt Fanny's letter to you," answered Fred, " and then you 'll know."

With eager haste the children sat themselves down on boxes and barrels; Mrs. Marble pushed up her wig, and pulled down her round iron-bound spectacles, to hear and see as sharply as possible; and clearing his voice with a great " hem ! " Fred read as follows : —

AUNT FANNY'S ANSWER.

" MY DEAR POP-GUN CHILDREN, —

" I should call you a set of little crazy cormorants, never to be satisfied, were I not rather pleased than otherwise by your asking me for a ' Sunday-story.' You are not the first one by a good many, and some of these days I mean to write a whole series of them. I was told that sixty-seven sets of ' Little Pet Books ' were ordered last winter by one Sunday-school, and forty by another. I know ' Night-caps,' ' Mittens,' and ' Socks ' are in some of the Sunday-schools too, and this makes me very happy.

" Oh, my darlings, I do so hope and pray that every year it pleases my Heavenly Father to permit me to live I shall write better than the last. There is a Chinese proverb which says, — ' With time and patience the mulberry-leaf becomes silk ; ' and an English one which declares that ' We may be as good as we please, if we please to be good.' I *do* please to *be* good, and to *do* good. Won't you pray that God will help me ?

" I send you with this your ' Sunday-story.' It does not differ in style from many others I have written, because I have made the children in it natural ; and so of course they are by no means any better than — than — you are."

Here Fred set up a loud laugh, and said, — " Hurrah ! Aunt Fanny ! Now we 'll see what we are like."

The rest laughed heartily also, and greatly enjoyed Mrs. Marble's chuckling, and saying, under her breath, " Why, look here, they 'll be extreeordinary bad, if young Dandelion is a pattern."

"But if it will strengthen you" (Fred read on) " in a determination to resist every temptation to do wrong, and renew your desire to love and obey the commands of your Maker, I shall be so glad, — so glad.

" I send you a beautiful little hymn, which I beg you to learn, and feel in your inmost heart when you say it. Here it is : —

" Mary's love may I possess,
Lydia's tender-heartedness,
Peter's ardent spirit feel,
James's faith by works reveal ;
Like young Timothy, may I
Every sinful passion fly.

" Most of all, may I pursue
That example Jesus drew ;
By my life and conduct show
How He lived and walked below ;
Day by day, through grace restored,
Imitate my Blessed Lord.

" Give my kindest regards to your dear papa
and mamma, and that nice old lady who keeps
the Post-office, and thinks you such a tease, —
in which she is quite right, — and believe me
ever your loving   " AUNT FANNY."

" Why, Aunt Fanny has sent her regards to
you! " cried all the children.

" Why, look here, so she has," returned
Mrs. Marble, her face all smiles. " I 'm beginning to like your Aunt Fanny. I wonder
what kind of a story she 's writ for you."

" Why, we 'll ask you to come and hear it,"
cried little Bob.

" Yes, do ! " exclaimed all the rest, — " next
Sunday evening."

" Bless your good little hearts ! so I will,
if your ma and pa will let me."

" We 'll ask them," said Kitty, " and send
you word."

So bidding her a merry good-bye, they
skipped and danced away, — but not before

Mrs. Marble had given little Bob a picture she had hanging up over the mantelpiece, in her room back of the shop, of "Samuel praying," — which delighted him to such a degree that he threw his arms round her neck and kissed her so heartily that he knocked her spectacles off and tilted her wig over her left ear. But, never mind; she was just as much pleased, and stood at the door and nodded at them till they turned a corner of the road.

THE PICTURE MRS. MARBLE GAVE LITTLE BOB.

Sunday came, — a soft, shining day, — and the little birds sang their hymns of praise all through the leafy trees.

The children went to church with their parents morning and afternoon, and then gathered round the tea-table talking pleasantly. The sweet breath of honeysuckles came in through the open windows; bird after bird flew by in the golden sunset air, chirping " Good-night "; the bees were hurrying home laden with honey, and all the sweet little whispering, drowsy insect-sounds, which are only heard in the country as God made it, came gently breaking through the stillness.

Many a time did the little feet of the younger children go pattering down the stone path of the garden, so that they might peep out in the lane to see if Mrs. Marble, who had been invited by their mamma, was in sight; and when she did appear, such a wild burst of joy broke from them, that the elder ones had to run out too; and the good old lady arrived in the midst of a sort of triumphal procession, quite breathless and rather flustered.

But the kind greeting of the children's parents soon put her at her ease; and when she sat down with them in her nice black silk dress, which her good son Gam, the blacksmith, had given her seven years ago, she looked, as Fred said, " like a perfect old darling."

It was intensely interesting to the children to observe the careful manner in which Mrs. Marble took out of her pocket an immense red silk pocket-handkerchief, unfolded it, and spread it over her lap, and the anxiety with which she made sure that it was twitched square and straight, and then to see her give her wig a little pull on the right side, and a little pull on the left, and settle her iron-bound spectacles firmly on the bridge of her nose.

It was perfectly delightful, after all this was done, to notice that she folded her hands, turning her thumbs over and over each other inside of them, and finally to hear her remark, with an amiable smile, — "Look here, I'm all ready; when are you going to begin?"

"I want to know, too," said little Bob.

"So do I! and so do I!" cried Kitty and Peter.

So Fred joyfully ran to the table-drawer, took out the manuscript, and with the warm sunset light glowing on the page, began to read "THE SUNDAY STORY."

NELLY RIVERS' GREAT RICHES.

A SUNDAY STORY.

———————

CHAPTER I.

DISCONTENT.

NELLY RIVERS was *so* tired of that room! She had counted every spot in the dark-blue ingrain carpet. She had gazed wearily upon the bare blue-painted walls, and blue chintz-covered furniture, the plainest of its kind, until her great dark eyes fairly ached for the sight of something pretty.

The room was the parlor of her father's parsonage, for Mr. Rivers was a clergyman. The ministers of some rich city-churches find it hard to live upon six or seven thousand dollars a year, and expect to have their houses refurnished and themselves sent to Europe every two or three years besides; and it is not to be wondered at if Mr. Rivers was unable to buy beautiful furniture with only six *hundred* dollars a year for his salary.

If the things of this world were all that Christians had to hope for or desire, little Nelly would not have been to blame in wishing for some pretty picture or tasteful ornament to brighten up the plain rectory parlor. She was an imaginative little body, with a great admiration for beauty in every shape; so it came to pass that in her eyes the scantily furnished room and dusty village street so close to the door, which formed the only view from the window, were rather forlorn.

There she sat, her hands folded listlessly, until at last out came a loud "Oh, dear! I am so tired of this ugly old house! I almost wish it would burn up."

The door leading from the parlor to the study was ajar. As Nelly said these words, it suddenly opened, and Mr. Rivers' kind, smiling face looked down upon her.

"Why, what a dreadful wish!" he said, coming towards her, and taking a handful of her shining curls in his grasp. "What can be the matter with my little Nelly?"

"Oh, I'm tired of everything, papa."

"Everything?" repeated her father. "That is a terrible feeling in a grand, beautiful world like this, which God has made and called 'very good.' I did hope you were not tired of *me*, for one thing."

"Oh, no, papa," cried Nelly, earnestly. "I love you dearly;" and she gave his hand a loving little squeeze against her cheek.

"Well, is it either of your brothers or baby-sister?"

"Oh, no, no, papa! that is not what I meant; I never could get tired of you, or dear mamma, or my sister or brothers, — but this room — it's so stupid! If we only had some pretty pictures to hang up, or some vases, or great looking-glasses and beautiful curtains, all lace and gold, like Mrs. Gray's. I do wish I was rich."

"Come here, my little girl," said Mr. Rivers, and he led Nelly gently into the study, which was at the back of the house, and seating himself in his arm-chair, took her on his knee. Then looking gravely in her face, he said, — " So, if God had seen fit to give you wealth, you would selfishly and foolishly spend it on worthless ornaments which could be of no possible service ? Do you believe this is the right use of money, Nelly ? "

" Well, maybe not, papa."

" I think I am a very happy man, yet there are certainly no pictures in my room," continued her father, smiling. " If I want a painting, only see what a beautiful one I have there ! "

He pointed, as he spoke, from the study-

window, to where a glimpse of the blue river
could be seen shining through the yellow-green
leaves of the willows, and the white spire of
the village church, with its golden arrow on
top, made a bright spot in the pleasant summer
sunlight.

Nearer by, Nelly's two little brothers were
watching with· delight some young ducks who
were waddling about and tumbling sideways
into a small pond. Behind them two little
dogs were frolicking, pretending to bite each
other's ears off, and barking such funny, quick
barks that it must have been laughing, dog-
fashion, while in the distance could be seen the
large handsome mansion in which Flora Gray
lived.

Nelly looked through the blinds at all this in
silence. The study-window was at the back
of the house, and the view was really a peaceful, charming scene; so, when Mr. Rivers
asked, "Don't you call that pretty, Nelly?"

she was forced in truth to answer, " Yes, papa."

" Then, if you have such a lovely picture painted by the hand of God, you surely need not be unhappy because you cannot buy the inferior work of men's hands."

" I suppose not," said Nelly, in a hesitating tone.

" Then, what is it you want so' much, little daughter ? "

" Well now, let me tell you, papa. Of course I would give to the poor, if I was rich; but there are so many things that rich people can do and have besides ! Yesterday, mamma sent me with a note to Mrs. Gray's, at Woodlawn, and while I waited for her to answer it, Flora Gray showed me all her pretty things. You don't know what a beautiful baby-doll she has ! — almost as large as sister Bessie, — and such a sweet little cradle for it ! and a whole bookcase to herself, full of story-books; and that

morning her papa had given her a box of sugar-
plums, as big as your sermon paper-box ! such
good ones ! Then the room was so beautifully
furnished, and Flora had on such a pretty
dress ! But just as we were beginning a nice
play, Mrs. Gray finished her note, and I had
to go; for though Flora begged me to stay, I
knew I must come home right away and take
care of the children. Now, if we were like the
Grays, mamma could have a nurse, and I could
have pretty dresses and dolls too; — and, oh
dear papa! then you need not write so hard
and long, and if anybody gave you the least
nice little thing, you need not send it right
away to some sick person; " here Nelly paused
rather suddenly in her torrent of talk, for she
saw that her father was looking both surprised
and somewhat grieved.

"Ah, now we come at the root of the matter," he said. "My Nelly is fretting and
making herself unhappy because she has the

care of her little brothers and sister a part of the day, and because Flora Gray has more playthings and books than herself! Would she be willing to let poor old Aunt Betsy, or the lame shoemaker, want the comforts that I can give them, so that I might take the money and buy toys and fine clothes for her? Does she feel as if her mother was imposing cruelly upon her, by asking her little girl's assistance in a few of very many cares?"

Nelly blushed deeply, and hung down her head. " I am sorry I was so ungrateful and naughty, papa," she murmured at last; "please forgive me! Indeed I will never be so bad again! I did feel when I was coming from Flora's as if I was an ill-used little girl,— and — I 'm afraid I was cross to Willie afterwards. Oh, papa, I am sorry!" and she burst into tears.

Mr. Rivers drew her gently to his breast and kissed her cheek. Then he said, in a sorrowful tone, — " My darling, you are envious of those better off than yourself; did you ever think that poor old bedridden Aunt Betsy and the lame shoemaker could with the same feeling wonder why you or I should be more prosperous and happy than they? Would you care to be like Aunt Betsy? "

" Oh dear, no! papa."

" Then you think God has been kinder to you than to her? "

" Oh, papa, I see I have been very wicked."

" Yes, Nelly, guilty of envy and discontent: two terrible sins. Pray to be delivered from them; let your entreaty be, — ' Create in me a new heart, O God, and renew a right spirit within me.' God will help you to conquer these sinful feelings. Now, would you like me to show you God's way to become rich? "

" Why, yes, papa," answered the little girl, looking up in his face with wondering eyes. " I did not know the Bible told us anything about that."

Mr. Rivers took a Testament from his desk, and opening it at the First Epistle of Paul to Timothy, pointed out these words, — " *God-liness is great riches.*"

" Does that mean that if we are good, it is just the same as being rich ? " asked Nelly.

" Read the rest of the verse," answered her father ; and she repeated " Godliness is great riches, *if a man be content with that he hath.*"

" Oh," said Nelly, pondering, with her finger on her lip ; " we must be *content* then ; that is the reason old Aunt Betsy is so thankful and happy the whole time. She is content, — is n't she ? "

" Yes ; whatever God pleases to give her is *just right.* ' Thy will be done,' is her heart's prayer. Make it your's, little Nelly, and you will care less and less for the perishing riches of this world, and more and more for that everlasting treasure which ' neither moth nor rust doth corrupt.' Will you try to do this ? "

" Yes, papa," said Nelly, softly.

" Well, then, suppose we make a plan for you, little daughter. When you find yourself feeling discontented, remember the text and try to gain that 'godliness' which is better than all the gold and silver in the world. Promise me to try this for a whole year, and at the end we will see how it has succeeded, and whether poor little Nelly Rivers has not become a very rich little girl."

The child's eyes filled with tears. She did not speak, but curled her arms round her father's neck and gave him a " good hug "; then slipping down from his knees, she ran out of the room and up-stairs to the nursery.

"BABY BESSIE WAS IN THE CRADLE." *Page* 39.

CHAPTER II.

TRYING TO BE GOOD.

MRS. RIVERS was seated near the window, sewing, — that never-ending sewing of mothers with young children.   Rover, a great dog, lay at her side, one paw folded over the other, lazily winking at the flies, and baby Bessie, who was just a year old, was in her cradle, — her blue eyes wide open, watching the bright spots of sunlight on the wall, and pretending to be trying to go to sleep as soon as possible ; but though she was quite good and quiet as long as her mother rocked the cradle with her foot, the moment she chanced to stop, a pitiful wail was set up, two chubby legs were raised, and off went the pretty white blanket, kicked on the floor.

Here was a chance for Nelly.   " Mamma,"

said she, " you go into the next room with your work, and I will rock Bessie and sing her to sleep."

As the baby made no objection to this arrangement, Mrs. Rivers went softly out, first kissing Nelly and giving her a glance so·full of love that the child's heart thrilled with happiness. Some of the "riches" had come already.

She ran to a closet and took out her own dear doll, and laid it in the cradle beside little Bessie, who hugged it to her little breast with delight; then softly rocking, she sang in her sweet voice this little song : — *

> " Little white Lily
> Sat by a stone
> Drooping and waiting
> Till the sun shone.

> " Little white Lily
> Sunshine has fed,

* G. M. McDonald.

Little white Lily
  Is lifting her head.

" Little white Lily
    Said, — ' It is good ;
It is white Lily's
    Clothing and food.'

" Little white Lily
    Is drest like a bride !
Shining with whiteness
    And crownèd beside.

" Little white Lily
    Droopeth for pain,
Waiting and waiting
    For the wet rain.

" Little white Lily
    Holdeth her cup,
Rain is fast falling
    And filling it up.

" Little white Lily
    Said, — ' Good again,
When I am thirsty
    To have the nice rain.

" ' Now I am stronger,
    Now I am cool ;
  Heat cannot burn me,
    My veins are so full '

" Little white Lily
    Smells very sweet ;
  On her head, sunshine,
    Rain at her feet.

" Thanks to the sunshine,
    Thanks to the rain !
  Little white Lily
    Is happy again ! "

Long before the pretty song was finished,
the baby's eyelids began to creep down over
her blue eyes, and soon she was in a sound,
quiet sleep.

Then Nelly stepped on the very tips of her
little toes into the next room and whispered to
her mother, — " Can I help you, dear mamma ?
Bessie is fast asleep."

" You may mend these stockings of your
brothers, dear," she answered, lifting a bundle
from the heaped-up work-basket beside her.

A great frown gathered in Nelly's face, and her mouth opened to ask in a fretful tone, — " What ! *all* those ? " when she checked herself, and saying in her heart this little prayer, — " Dear Jesus, help me to be good, " she spoke out cheerfully, — " Yes, mamma, I will do them right away ; " and bringing her little chair and basket, she sat down with the big bundle of stockings, determined to mend them every one.

Her two little brothers, tired of watching the young ducks, had come into this room. One was crawling about the floor, looking for pins. His mamma had promised to give him a penny for fifty pins, and he found quite a number every day. The other little fellow was very busy. cutting paper with a pair of old scissors, saying he was making a paper elephant for the baby.

Presently he got tired of making elephants, and throwing down his scissors, he ran to the back of Nelly's chair, and climbing up with great difficulty, put his chubby arms around her neck, reached down and snatched the stocking out of her hand.

"Come, play with me," he said.

"Nelly must do her work," said his mother.

"But I *so* tired," pleaded little Willie.

"And I can't find any more pins," said Maitland, who was called "Maity," for short.

"Well, then," said his mamma, "shall I tell you all a story?"

This delightful offer was received with such a shout of joy, that Nelly had to run into the next room, to rock the cradle, for fear the baby might wake up in a fright; but the dear little thing only opened one eye, and the next moment was just as sound asleep as before.

The good child came softly back, and Mrs. Rivers said, — "What shall the story be about?"

Nelly thought a moment, with her finger

on her lip; then she said, — "About when you was a little girl, mamma."

"Oh, yes, yes!" chimed in the boys, their eyes sparkling; and she began as you will read in the next chapter.

CHAPTER III.

MRS. RIVERS' STORY.

" When I was a little girl, my father said to me, one pleasant summer morning, — ' I 'm going to Newburgh, on business, and you may go with me if you choose.'

" You may be sure I was perfectly delighted, and skipped off to tell my mother and get ready."

" Where was I then ? " asked Willie, in a grieved tone. " Why did n't you take *me* ? "

Nelly laughed merrily at this question, and her mother smiled, as she replied, — "You were not in the world at all, or I should certainly have taken such a dear little tot with me on my excursion."

" Oh, would you ? " said Willie, much comforted; and Mrs. Rivers continued, — "So my father had the old rockaway brought to the door, mother kissed me, and bid me be a good girl, and brother Robert, who was a great tease, pretended to be crying his eyes almost out with grief at my departure. Meanwhile, father put a basket in the rockaway that had in it two white bantam chickens, and stood waiting for me to come."

"Grandpa Woodward was n't a farmer, — was he?" asked Nelly.

"No; but he was very proud of his chickens, and he meant to give these to a minister in town, whom we were going to visit."

Mrs. Rivers had lost both her father and mother when she was a young girl, and her children were always very much interested to know about the dear grandma and grandpa, whom they could never see on earth.

Nelly's question answered, her mother went on with the story, thus: — "We rode along

for some time in silence, and then I began
to ask some questions.

"'How far is it to Newburgh, father?' I
said.

"'About fourteen miles,' he replied.

"'Fourteen miles! oh, what a long way!
Will it take us all day to get there?'

"'Why, no,' said my father, laughing; 'we
shall get there in about two hours and a half.'

"'Do people who go to see ministers always
have to take 'em chickens?' was my next
question.

"'I'm sure I don't know,' said father, laughing again. 'I am going to give these bantams
to Mr. Russell, because I know he can't get
such another pair out of my hen-house.' Here
the two chickens gave such a 'Cluck, cluck!'
together, as much as to say, 'That's a fact.'

"Presently we came to a toll-house, and had
to stop and pay two or three cents toll. There
was an old gray cat sunning herself on the

window-seat, with three little kittens nestled up against her. One had a blue ribbon tied round its neck, the second a pink, and the third, a red ribbon.

" ' Oh, what *dear* little things ! ' I cried.

" ' Would you like to have one, Miss ?' asked the toll-keeper's wife.

" ' Oh ! may I, papa ? ' I exclaimed.

" ' You can take one if you choose, Nelly,' he replied; ' but don't you think it will be rather in the way ? '

" ' Why, papa, a dear little kitten *could n't* be in the way. May I have the one with the white nose ? ' "

" Why ! was your name Nelly, too ? " interrupted Nelly, opening her eyes wide.

" My name is Nelly now," answered her mother, smiling.

" Oh, no, it is n't. Papa calls you ' Pussy.' "

" Well, that is a pet name, just as I call you my little robin."

"Oh," said Nelly; and she jumped up to give her mother a little affectionate squeeze round her neck, and whisper, — "I'm so dreadful glad your name is Nelly. I love you, mamma."

Mrs. Rivers kissed the dear little girl, and then went on with her story.

"The good-natured woman gave me the kitten with the white nose, and I kissed and thanked her, and off we rode. The poor little thing did n't seem very happy at being carried off from its mother, and mewed piteously at first, but after a while it cuddled itself down in my lap and went sound asleep.

"We had a pleasant ride to town, and when we rattled at last over the stones of the streets, I was very much interested in looking at the numbers of people, and the shops, which seemed quite grand to a little country girl like me. Presently we drew up at a confectioner's, and my father stopped the wagon, and went in to buy me a luncheon."

" What did he bring you ? " asked Nelly.

" He brought me some lemon-cakes, and some rusk, and a turn-over pie."

" Oh, how good ! I wish you had taken me ! " cried both Willie and Maity.

" Next time I go, I will," said Mrs. Rivers, laughing.

" Very well," answered Willie. " Then what did grandpa do ? "

" He got in the rockaway again, and we drove to a saddler's, where he stopped once more.

" ' Now, Nelly,' he said, ' I am going to be here some time; do you think you will be afraid to stay in the wagon alone ? '

" ' Oh, no, father ! I should like to stay here very much.'

" ' Very well,' he said. ' I will fasten Lennox, (that was the horse,) so he cannot get away, and be back as soon as possible.'

" So saying, he entered the saddler's store. There were blue blinds to the lower part of the window, and the door was made of thick, rough glass, so that it was not very easy to look out, I suppose, and impossible to see in.

" There I sat, munching my cake and nursing my kitten, quite contented and happy.

" Presently a very odd-looking old man came along. He was dressed in dirty, ragged clothes, and had a long peacock's feather, and some flying paper-streamers fastened to his broken straw hat, for the poor old fellow was crazy.

" I was looking at him, and wondering what could be the matter with him, when all at once he came up close to the rockaway and stared in.

" ' Ho! little gal!' he said, in a hoarse voice, grinning at me, — ' what 's that? cake?'

" I was terribly frightened, but managed to stammer out, — 'Yes, sir.'

" ' What do you mean by calling me *sir !* ' he exclaimed, in a sudden, angry tone. ' How

dare you? Give me that cake! it's mine!'
And before I could help it, he snatched my turn-
over pie, and ate it up at two mouthfuls."

"Oh! what *did* you do?" exclaimed Nelly,
breathlessly. "What a dreadful old man!"

"Poor mamma! Maity so sorry!" said
little Maity.

"I was so frightened," continued Mrs.
Rivers, "that I stared at him without saying
a word, — then I exclaimed, — 'Oh, please
don't, — please go away!' and began to cry.

"'Then give me some more cake!' said
the silly creature, fiercely, 'or I'll get in
the wagon and ride you off to the moon! The
man in the moon knows me, and he's very
fond o' fat little gals! Ow!' and he made a
sort of snap at me with his mouth wide open.

"'Oh, take it all, — only go away!' I cried;
and I held out all the rusk and cakes I had
had, except the one I had eaten, — and, hiding
my face in my hands, cried harder than ever."

"Why did n't somebody see him and stop him?" asked Nelly, half crying herself.

"Partly, my dear child, because in a large town, people seem to think of no one but themselves. No matter what happens in the street, if a little child is being abused, or a lady injured, nine people out of ten will think, 'Oh, it's none of my business,— I sha' n't interfere;' and they walk on, like the Priest and Levite of old, without caring what becomes of the poor traveller. Besides, the old man was well known in Newburgh, and no one thought him likely to do any harm, I suppose."

"Well, — go on, — please," said all the children at once.

"As I told you, I hid my face in my hands, and wished for my father. Suddenly I heard a loud shout of 'Hoo! Hurray!' the wagon was jerked suddenly forwards, — I raised my head, and found the old man had untied Lennox, and was shouting at the top of his voice to set him running!

" The poor terrified horse started off at full speed, I holding to the sides of the rockaway and screaming for help. I fortunately remembered what father once told me, never to try to get out of a wagon when a horse was running away, or I might have been killed. The boys shouted, people on the sidewalks stopped to stare at the show, and several men ran after the rockaway, trying to catch the dragging reins, and shouting 'Whoa!' at the tops of their voices. This only frightened Lennox more than ever, and in his terror he turned the corner of another street, and rushed down that, till we were far away from the place where I had left father, and yet seemed no more likely to stop than at first, — particularly as the crowd followed us and increased by the way. At last, not seeming to see where he was going, Lennox ran right up against a large country wagon, struck one of the shafts against it, and broke· it directly in two! The shock stopped

him, and one of the men catching the reins at
the same moment, guided him to the sidewalk.
Of course everybody else stopped to see the
fun, on the spot; — a crowd of little boys
stared and grinned at me, — and one, more
kind-hearted than the rest, climbed up on the
carriage-step, and offered me a very sticky bit
of candy to comfort me, saying, — 'Don't
cry, Sissy; here, take that.'

"But I could not take the candy. I was too
frightened. I only hugged my kitty, who all
this time had been clinging to my dress with its
little claws, and mewing piteously, and sobbed
out, — 'Oh, please take me back to father!
oh, please take me back to father!'

"'Where is your father?' asked the man
who had stopped the horse, in a kind voice.

"'He went in a saddler's shop, sir, — a shop
with blue blinds, and a kind of thick glass
door; and then the old crazy man came and
untied Lennox! Oh, dear, dear!'"

Here Little Willie, who was very sensitive, and had been listening to the story with quivering lips and tearful eyes, exclaimed " Oh, dear ! " too, and, hiding his face against Nelly's shoulder, began to cry very hard.

" Why, don't cry, little boy ! " said his mother, cheerily. " It is all over now, and you see I got off quite safely, or I should not be here to tell you the story, — should I ? "

" Oh, but Willie so sorry ! " said the child, looking up in his mother's face.

" Shall I stop the story, then ? "

" Oh, no ! please go on, mamma. I won't cry any more."

" Well, when I gave this description of the saddler's store, the man said, — ' Oh, I guess it 's Hartley's ; I can take you there.' So he sent one of the staring boys into a shop for a piece of stout cord, and having tied the broken shaft together as well as he could, he got in the rockaway, and drove Lennox slowly back the way we had come.

" My father met us on the road ; he had heard
the noise in the street, and rushed out of the
saddler's just in time to see Lennox disappear
round the corner. I can't tell you how glad he
was to find me unhurt, nor how, as he hugged
me up to his breast and kissed me twenty times,
he declared over and over that he would never
leave his little Nelly alone again. He thanked
the kind man for bringing me back, and wanted to give him some money, as he looked poor,
but he would not take it, and so we bid him
good-bye and left him."

" Then did you go to the minister's ? " asked
Nelly.

" Yes ; we drove there directly, and found
them just sitting down to dinner, thinking we
were not coming. Kitty and I had as much roast
lamb and mashed potatoes as we could eat, —
and hungry enough we were, I can tell you."

" Oh, I so glad you had lamb ! " said Willie.

" Then, after that, what do you think we had
for dessert ? " said Mrs. Rivers, smiling.

"What?" asked the children in a breath.

"Why, turn-over pies! So I had one, after all."

"How nice! Well, what happened after that?" they all asked.

"I think the next thing was that my father went off to the blacksmith's to get the shaft of the rockaway patched somehow or other, and I went up-stairs with the minister's wife. I felt so tired and sleepy after my long ride and the fright, that, when Mrs. Russell asked me if I would like to lie down a short time, I said 'Yes, ma'am,' directly; and my head had hardly touched the pillow when I went fast asleep.

"About half-past five Mrs. Russell woke me gently, and told me father was ready to start. The rockaway was before the door, and in a few minutes we were in it once more, — with the empty basket riding in state on the back seat, and Kitty in my lap. It was a very close, sultry afternoon; and as we got out of Newburgh, and were toiling slowly along the up-hill road, my father said, — ' I rather wish I had waited an hour longer, Nelly; seems to me we are going to have a thunder-shower.'

" ' Oh, father,' I cried, ' a thunder-storm! how dreadful! Do please drive back, — I am so afraid of thunder.'

" Just as I spoke we heard the first distant peal, and saw the bright flash of lightning far away.

" ' Oh, papa! what shall we do?' I cried.

" ' Do?' said my father; ' why, go on, of course! Is it possible, Nelly, that you are afraid of thunder?'

" ' I guess I am!' I said.

" ' But, my dear child, if there were any danger, have you not faith to believe that God would protect you? A thunder-storm is a great benefit and blessing to the earth; and if God can keep the little birds and all other living creatures from harm, will he not care for you also?'

" ' But maybe the lightning will strike us ? '

" ' No ; it cannot harm us while there are no trees near us to attract it ; and as for the thunder, that is only a noise ; and you are not afraid of a noise, — are you ? '

" ' Why, no,' I said, beginning to laugh at my foolish terror. Just then, however, a much louder crash than before set me trembling again, and I hid my face against kitty's soft fur, while father got out of the rockaway, and, bidding me hold the reins, unfastened the leather curtains on each side and behind, and buttoned them down securely. Then he took the reins again, while I scrambled over to the back seat, and seating himself beside me, just as the first heavy drops pattered down, we drove along through the storm.

" I can never forget how kindly he soothed and talked away my silly terror at the thunder and lightning, instead of scolding me, as some fathers would have done, and told me some beautiful verses about a thunder-storm, which made me quite forget to be afraid."

" Won't you tell me the verses ? " said Nelly.

" I will if I can remember them. It is so long ago now, that I have nearly forgotten what they were. Let me think." Mrs. Rivers paused for a moment, and then said, — " Oh, now I believe I can repeat them. They are called

"THE LITTLE BOY AND THE THUNDER-STORM.

" ' The thunder-storm is coming !
I hear its distant roar !
Oh, hide me, sister, hide me quick,
Until its rage is o'er.

" ' The brilliant lightning blinds me !
I see the pouring rain ;
The thunder deafens me to hear, —
Hark ! there it comes again.

" ' Oh, take me, sister, on your lap,
And let me hide my eyes
Against your breast, who love me well,
Till shine the gloomy skies.

" ' For GOD is in the thunder,
I heard my nurse-maid say ;

It is his wrathful voice we hear; —
Oh, sister, let us pray!'

"'Nay, then, my darling brother,'
The loving sister said,
'If GOD is in the raging storm,
We need not be afraid.

"'His anger, like the thunder,
Comes pealing from above;
The lightning seems His awful eye, —
But ah! the *rain*'s His love.

"'It moistens and refreshes
The hot and thirsty plain,
Until the drooping corn and flowers
Are fresh and bright again.

"'The lightning purifieth,
Like sorrow's fearful shock;
It smites the noxious weeds of sin,
But cannot touch "our Rock."'

"Then, looking up to heaven, —
'Behold! His grace divine
Has made upon the brilliant blue
A bow of promise shine.

"'And His kind voice doth whisper —
"Weep, little one, no more;
My love has cleared the gloomy skies:
The thunder-storm is o'er!"'

"As my father finished these verses, the clouds broke away, the sun came out in all its splendor, and right before us we saw a magnificent rainbow!

"Oh, how it seemed to cheer and lighten my heart! I gave father a good hug and kiss for his kindness, and promised I would never again feel any foolish dread of a thunder-storm."

"And did n't you?" asked Nelly.

"No, never; if ever I began to have some of my tremors, I always repeated to myself, — 'But ah! the *rain*'s His love!' — and then I grew cheerful again."

"Well, what happened after that?"

"Why, after that, I and papa, and Kitty, and Lennox, and the basket, and the rockaway, all got home safe together, and had a famous tea of bread and milk, — that is, Kitty and I did. So there 's the end of my history-book, ro-rum, corum, torum!" said Mrs Rivers, smiling.

"And my stockings, too!" cried Nelly.

"Why, there were n't so many, after all! Thank you, mamma, for your story. I mean to learn that piece of poetry by heart, if you will copy it for me."

" Will you copy it for me, too?" said Willie.

" Oh, you little goose! you can't read yet!" cried Nelly.

" Am I a goose?" asked Willie, putting up his lip.

" I think your sister forgot when she said that," said Mrs. Rivers, gently.

Nelly blushed. " I am sorry, mamma. No, Willie, you are not a goose, and I will teach you the verses, if you like."

The little boy curled his chubby arms round his sister's neck. "I love you, Nelly," he said, softly; and the mother smiled sweetly on her good children.

It was now nearly dinner-time, and Mrs. Rivers went down-stairs to direct their one servant; while Nelly, looking in the next room, and seeing that the baby was still asleep, gave each of her little brothers a pencil and piece of paper, and sat down herself to read a nice new book which had been sent to her. It was called " The Standard-Bearer," and contained a letter from " Aunt Fanny."

This letter was written when Dr. Anthon, one of the best and purest of God's ministers, was alive, — not long after he went to sit forever at the feet of the Beloved Master, whom he had served so faithfully while here upon earth.

Nelly knew and loved " Aunt Fanny " dearly, so she read her letter the very first thing. Here it is.

No, here it is n't; because I think my " good little hearts " reading this will like to know, what I omitted to mention in the letter, — namely, that the children there spoken of had learned some verses in the Bible, besides their

Catechism; and as these verses were about a most touching incident in the life of our Saviour, which happened shortly before his death, I will repeat them here. They are from the gospel according to John, beginning at the twelfth verse.

" On the next day much people that were come to the feast, when they heard that Jesus was coming to Jerusalem,

" Took branches of palm-trees and went forth to meet him, and cried Hosanna; Blessed is the King of Israel that cometh in the name of the Lord.

" And Jesus, when he had found a young ass, sat thereon; as it is written,

" Fear not, daughter of Zion; behold thy king cometh, sitting on an ass's colt."

See, my darlings, how the prophecy was fulfilled which was written in the book of the Old Testament, called " Zechariah," ninth chapter, ninth verse, — written years and years before our Saviour was born.

Here it is : — " Rejoice greatly, O daughter
of Zion ; shout, O daughter of Jerusalem : behold, thy king cometh unto thee : he is just,
and having salvation ; lowly, and riding upon
an ass, and upon a colt, the foal of an ass."

This was on the first day of the week in
which our Saviour was crucified. He entered
Jerusalem, the Holy City, riding in this lowly
fashion, while the multitude waved palm-branch-
es before Him, and sang hosannas, strewing
their garments in his path.

And yet, before the week was out, the same
multitude cried, " Away with him ! crucify
him !" He knew this was to be, so he rode on
in a silence, full of grief.

On this day, also, Jesus scourged the money-
changers, and the buyers and sellers in the
Temple. He healed numbers of the sick, lame,
and blind ; and many of the chief priests did
in fact believe on Him, though they were afraid
to confess Him openly.

In the evening our Saviour returned to Bethany with the twelve apostles, and was probably the guest of Lazarus and his good and pious sisters.

Now I will give you the little story from the "Standard-Bearer." Every word is true; and it was *my* Alice who made the speech in church.

CHAPTER IV.

A LETTER FROM "AUNT FANNY," TELLING HOW ALICE SPOKE
IN CHURCH.

DEAR LITTLE FRIENDS, —

I AM almost certain you would like to hear
what happened in our church one pleasant
Sunday afternoon; and so I mean to tell you.

Dr. Anthon's class of dear little children had
gathered round his chair in the afternoon, to
say their Catechism for the last time that season. The beloved rector, after the services
were over and the rest of the people had left
the church, had seated himself, as usual, within
the chancel, with a pleasant smile upon his face,
and the little ones hastened up the aisles, and
knelt around the railings.

They had a pretty long task to recite, for
they had agreed to learn a hymn, — each to

select his or her favorite one, and as many as five verses long, — in addition to two pages of Catechism. No wonder one little girl said it was " quite a heap of lessons "; but, notwithstanding, she meant to " learn them all perfect." And so she did.

The hymns of the children were all beautiful, and all well recited; and tender and loving tears glistened in the eyes of the good mothers who sat near and listened.

When all the lessons were through, the kind rector made this little speech : —

" Children, you will remember I promised that *you* should decide what I was to do with your chancel offerings. I have a little memorandum here, which says you have given me five dollars and two cents. Now what shall I do with this money ? You know that there are foreign missions and home missions. One good minister told you, some time ago, what was doing in China, and it was very interesting;

and another one, a little while since, told you
what had been done in Africa. He said to me
afterwards that there were two young colored
men in Africa, who were very anxious to be
educated so as to become God's holy ministers
in their own country. It would require about
two hundred dollars to do it, and he was afraid
he would not be able to get the money. Then
I told him to take hope and comfort to his
heart, for I thought I could promise him the
money ; — and what do you think has happened ? Why, this very morning the congregation have given very nearly enough for this
excellent purpose, which makes me feel very
happy. Now, what do you say ? Shall your
money go with the other to educate the young
men ? Will you give it to Africa ? Who
says yes ? "

Then a thoughtful-looking, dark-eyed little
girl, whom Aunt Fanny calls Evangeline in
her heart, but whose real name is Mary, ran to

her father to know what she should do; and
Alice, another little one, whom you all know,
asked her mother, and when they turned back
they said, " Yes, sir, give it to Africa; " and
little Emma, the tiniest of the flock, said,
" Yes! " and Laura, after glancing her bright
eyes toward her mother, said, " Yes! " and the
good rector was looking very much pleased,
when, quite unexpectedly, Clara said, " *No!* "
and William, one of the brightest boys I
ever saw, said " *No!* " too, very decidedly
indeed.

What was to be done? The kind rector
looked puzzled, and the good mothers smiled
and whispered to each other that the children
knew perfectly well what they were about, and
meant to have this momentous business of giving their money to the missionaries settled to
their own minds; the only trouble was, they
were not all of *one* mind. This sometimes
happens with grown-up people, — but perhaps
I ought to have kept that a. secret.

"Well," said Dr. Anthon, pleasantly, "this is quite a difficulty; four against two. Still, I have great hopes for Africa."

Then Alice, in a sweet little piping, lisping voice, was heard to say, — "Dr. Anthon, suppose we divide the money *evenly*, and give half to Africa, and half to home missions, — would n't that be better?"

"Ah!" said the good rector, while a smile broke all over his face, "that 's an excellent idea! very good indeed; we will put it to vote." So he asked all the children one by one, and a joyful "Yes!" was the answer from all. They seemed so glad thus to settle the difficulty, and to help both; it was really delightful to think, that, if they *were* only little children, they could help along God's work: and thus their tiny offerings were doubly blessed.

"And now, children," said the rector, "I do not intend you shall learn Catechism when

we meet again, as some of you have been
through it more than once. I mean to form
you into a little Bible-class; — how would you
like that ? "

I only wish you could have seen the row of
dimples that came out on their bright little
faces when he said this!

Why, just think of it ! A Bible-class, like
great grown-up people ! It was perfectly delightful. They really began to think they
were not such little bodies after all; and when
the good minister had prayed a beautiful prayer,
asking a blessing upon the lessons they had
received, the little ones left the chancel, a joyful
happy group.

As they were walking down the aisle, Laura
turned her bright face up to her mother and
whispered, — "Mamma, I *did* wish to speak
right out, and say I wanted the money to go to
building the new Sunday-school, or else to be
given to the ' ten-cent fund,' to build a church
out West."

"Well, my dear," answered her mother, kindly, 'I think it will do just as much good where it *is* going;" which opinion completely dispelled the little girl's regret, and she was quite satisfied.

And Alice whispered to *her* mother, — "Oh, mamma! was n't it good that we divided the money *evenly*, because you know Africa might be jealous, — might n't she ?"

Her mother smiled at the word "jealous," and told her it was quite right to avoid any risk of that kind, as jealousy among Christians was a very sad thing.

I wish I could tell you all that Mary, and dear little Emma, and Clara, and that bright little fellow, William, said, — but my letter is already too long. Of this, you may be sure, they were all pleased, and loved their kind rector more than ever, and looked forward with delightful anticipations to the time when they would be his dear little Bible-class.

When that time comes, perhaps you may hear more about them from your loving

AUNT FANNY.

Ah! that good time never came! for the next year, just at the season when the dear little Bible-class would have been formed, Dr. Anthon went home to his Father in heaven.

"Coo, coo!" said a soft voice, just as Nelly was about to read the next story; and two little fat feet were raised up in the air, and the baby-blanket was kicked out of the cradle and over on the floor.

"Oh, you darling!" cried Nelly; "how you kick! I must pat your little toes."

She took hold of a chubby foot, and giving each little toe a shake in turn, said: —

> "This little pig went to market,
>   This little pig stayed at home;
>   This little pig had apple-dumpling,
>   This little pig had none;

This little pig said, 'squeak,
Squeak, squeak!' my apple-dumpling
Is as hard as a stone."

This tickled the baby very much, and she put out her other foot to be served the same way, when the dinner-bell rang.

Then Nelly took her up, brushed her few soft hairs, which made one darling little round curl at the back of her neck, and calling Willie and Maity, they went down to dinner.

All the afternoon the little girl tried to win some of those riches of which her father had told her. You see her resolution was fresh and strong, and this made it easy for her to be perfectly good all this first day. We shall see, as we go on with her story, whether this resolve remained steadfast through every trial and temptation.

CHAPTER V.

THE ROBBER-RABBITS

FLORA GRAY was very fond of Nelly. She was constantly sending for her to come to Woodlawn, which was the name of their beautiful place; and Nelly, I am sorry to relate, would be all smiles, skips, and happiness while there, but very often came home with an expression as if somebody had just thrown a glass of cold water in her face.

There were so many delightful things at Woodlawn. Besides Flora's playthings, of which there seemed no end, there were swans swimming gracefully on the beautiful little lake; peacocks strutting up and down, displaying their gorgeous tails; a pet lamb, who would eat out of your hand; little white bantams, who looked as if they had ruffled pantalets on; and three pretty lop-eared rabbits, which Nelly never grew tired of feeding. It was not strange, therefore, that the little girl should like to go to see Flora, — and perhaps we ought not to blame her for sometimes wishing she could live as Flora did.

In the very next house to Woodlawn dwelt a sharp-featured, cross-grained, old fellow whose name was Squire Dusenberry. He seemed to think that his eyes were made for nothing but to look as cross as possible at everybody, and his mouth for no other purpose but to eat and scold. There were man-traps and spring-guns all over his place, to catch trespassers; and you could not enter the gate without a big dog making a rush at you, and trying to snap at your legs. If you screamed with fright, Squire Dusenberry would come out smacking his lips, and say, " Guess you a'n't fond of dogs; " and that was all the comfort you got.

One unlucky Friday, one of the pet rabbits belonging to Flora found a small round hole in

the fence between Squire Dusenberry's grounds
and Woodlawn.   He immediately called a mass-
meeting of the rest of the rabbits, and proposed
that they should burrow under this hole, and
find out what was on the other side.

" My friends," he said, standing up on his
hind-legs and eagerly erecting his ears, — " my
friends, I think I smell something remarkably
nice on the other side of this fence. I 'm quite
tired of staying here forever, and having my

meals regularly served up four times a day like two-legged animals. Come, let's hunt up a dinner for ourselves."

On this, a fat old white rabbit, as round as a dumpling, turned her back, observing, "That little cat of a rabbit wants to get us all into mischief. I had my paw well pinched once when I poked my nose where I had no business to go. *I* shall stop at home."

But the others were overjoyed at the chance for an adventure. They did not pay the slightest attention to the sensible remarks of the old rabbit, but began with might and main to throw up the dirt under the hole in the fence.

Merrily they worked, — their long ears twisting and turning every which way, ready to scamper off and hide, if the gardener or Flora or her brother Charley should come that way. But nothing happened, and at last the hole was large enough for them to squeeze through.

How perfectly enchanting! They were in

the very middle of Squire Dusenberry's cabbage-bed. Nothing could be more splendid or complete to the eyes and appetite of a rabbit. Just imagine, my good little hearts, your having a present of a whole barrel-full of candy, and you will know how perfect this was.

In the greatest glee the robber-rabbits commenced eating, and made such a prodigious snip, snip, snipping! that the fat old rabbit heard them distinctly, and, what is more, she smelt such a delightful odor, that her very whiskers curled up, and her ears seemed starting out of her head.

" I can't afford to lose all the fun," she said
to herself; so she quietly wriggled through the
hole in the fence. She gave a start of delight
when she saw the lovely green cabbages sitting
up so round and crisp in every direction; after
which, you may be sure, the old soul never
waited for the dinner-bell to ring, but fell to
eating as bold as a lion, just as if all the cabbages belonged to her, and she had nothing to
do but to help herself.

And now all the rabbits were so absorbed in
this delightful employment that they did not
hear old Squire Dusenberry shuffling along in
his carpet slippers, coming to see and admire
his fine vegetable garden.

All at once he observed two large white
ears waving back and forth. " Hullo ! " he exclaimed, softly, " if it a'n't them plaguy rabbits
from Woodlawn eating up my very best cabbages ! I 'll fix 'em ! "

Breathing hard with rage, he shuffled back

to the house, marched up into his bedroom, and took down his double-barrelled gun. It was already loaded with shot enough to kill a dozen rabbits. Then he came out again so softly that the poor things did not hear him, or else they might have given the alarm to each other by thumping on the ground with one of their hind-feet.

BANG.!! BANG!!

With a cry like a human being, two of the rabbits leaped up in the air and fell dead! while the poor old white rabbit lay panting and bleeding on the ground, both of her forelegs broken by some of the cruel shot.

Then this terrible old Squire, what does he do but tie all three up by the hind-legs, with a piece of twine he took out of his pocket, and hang them over the fence, — a warning, he said, to evil-doers.

The old white rabbit soon died, drawing long gasping breaths; and there the three hung so still, — their long ears stiffened back, their large prominent eyes without lustre, only fit now to be made into a pie. It was really dreadful !

CHAPTER VI.

REVENGE.

THE next day being Saturday, Nelly was invited to spend it at Woodlawn; and as she had sincerely tried to be a good child all the week, her kind mother gave her permission to go.

With joyful skips and bounds the happy little girl soon arrived at the great house; and of course the first thing to be done was to go and visit all the pets. The beautiful swans were coaxed to come up and be fed with cake; the peacocks were begged to display their splendid tails; the pet lamb was hugged and kissed; and then Flora, Charley, and Nelly went to look for the pretty white rabbits.

They looked and looked. "Why, where can they be?" they asked of each other.

"Perhaps they have got into the stable," said

Charley, "and are feeding with the horses. What fun! to see them trying to chew up long straws, which will only tickle their whiskers. Come, let's go."

Off they ran to the stable, and looked into all the mangers; then they climbed and scrambled up a ladder into the hay-loft, and forgot the rabbits for a little while, racing around in the greatest glee, and tumbling the hay about in a way that made the loft look as if a regiment of disorderly rats had all built their nests in it; — and no doubt its condition set the head-groom half crazy the next time he went there.

"Isn't this jolly!" cried Charley, turning head-over-heels into a great pile of sweet-smelling hay.

"Perfectly lovely," said Nelly, tumbling down in a heap beside him, — her curls tossed all over her face, and bits of straw sticking up in them in every direction; while Flora was trying to walk up what she called "Straw

Hill," and fell over on her nose at every step, screaming and laughing with delight, and creating such a dust that all three were seized with a tremendous fit of sneezing, which, with the laughing and screaming, seemed enough to take the roof off, and frightened all the horses below into kicking-fits.

At last, breathless with fun, they sat down close together in the hay, and began to wonder again what had become of the rabbits.

Presently Flora jumped up and looked through a round window at the back of the loft.

The sun was shining brightly upon some white object which seemed hanging over the fence at the very end of the lawn.

" What can it be ? " she thought to herself. " Come here, Nell ! — come, Charley ! " she called. " That can't be Bunny, 'way down there, — can it ? "

" Should n't wonder," answered her brother. " Let 's go and see."

Up they jumped, and down the ladder they hurried, nearly breaking their necks, and scampered as fast as possible to the very end of the green lawn, and rushed pell-mell up to the poor white rabbits.

For one instant they stood quite still, astonishment and grief depicted in their faces; then Charley, springing up on the fence and looking over, saw the half-eaten cabbages. He understood it at once, and jumping down, his face crimson with rage, stamping his foot, he cried out, — "That abominable old Squire Dusenberry has shot them! I know he has! I could beat him to powder! Ugh! I could *scrunch* him!"

"The hateful thing!" exclaimed Flora, bursting into tears.

"The bad, cruel man!" said Nelly, also crying with all her might.

"I'll do something to him! I'll kill something *he* loves; I'll — I'll. Oh, I'll fix

him !" cried Charley, growing more and more
angry, as he tenderly lifted the poor rabbits
down. "Just as if he could n't spare two or
three of his old cabbage-heads !"

"I wish somebody would eat *his* head," said
Flora.

"Oh, dear me !" sighed Nelly, "what
can we do to him ?"

Charley untied the string with which the
hind-legs of his favorites were fastened; and
each taking one, the children walked slowly
back to the stable.

At the door they met Sam the stable-boy,
and, all talking together, informed him of
Squire Dusenberry's shameful conduct.

Sam rubbed the cuff of his coat over his dirty
face two or three times, to hide a grin, while
the dismal fate of the poor rabbits was related
to him ; then, as he was a regular Yankee, and
was always for getting the most out of everything, he said, "Wal, Master Charley, I don't

see no occasion to feel so desput bad about this
here; rabbit-pie is first-rate feedin', and the
critturs had got to come to it sooner or later."

"Oh, you awful boy!" exclaimed Flora.
"Do you suppose we can eat our poor rabbits?"

"No indeed!" cried Charley; "we are going
to bury them. Come, Sam, get the spade and
dig a grave for us."

"Oh, Miss Flora! they are so very plump!
just feel their backs," — and Sam lifted poor
Bunny and began pinching her.

"Let her alone, you wicked boy!" screamed
Flora. "We are going to bury her, — the
others too. Put on your spectacles, if you 've
got any, and find a nice box for us, and then
hurry and dig a grave."

Sam grinned again; and then going into the
barn, he brought out an empty old box which
had "Babbit's Premium Soap" pasted on the
side, on a flaming red paper. Some hay was

put in the bottom, and the three rabbits were laid in Babbitt's soap-box, side by side, — the children looking on with quivering lips; then the top was nailed on by Sam, who always kept his tools in the barn; a hole was dug under a tree, and the box was put in and carefully covered up.

The three children, with anger still burning in their hearts, then went and sat down on a green bank, talking over their wrongs till the dinner-bell rang.

Of course, the violent death of the rabbits was the only topic of conversation at the table, and Charley's papa promised to have a very solemn talk with Squire Dusenberry about his conduct.

"Tell him I *hate* him!" cried Charley, his eyes flashing. "Tell him I'll get our swans to hiss at him, he's so mean!"

"Oh, Charley!" said his mother, "don't talk so. You must learn to forgive those who

despitefully use you.   Remember your rabbits
were stealing the Squire's cabbages, and no
doubt he was very angry, and perhaps he is
sorry enough now."

"Yes, but that won't bring them back; he
ought to have been sorry first."

His father laughed at this comical way of
stating the case, and the children ran off to
play.

But somehow, though they tried to enjoy
themselves, and Flora had every one of her
dolls out in the arbor and gave them a party,
the sad fate of the rabbits would come into
their minds every moment, and steal all the
dimples out of their faces.

All of a sudden Charley sprung up, with an
exclamation of, "I'll do it! see if I don't!"

"Do what?" cried both the girls, staring
at him in astonishment.

"*I* know! *I'll* do it!" said Charley, again
shaking his head fiercely. "I'll fix him! He
won't shoot rabbits again in a hurry!"

"Oh, the Squire you mean!" cried the girls. "Tell us what you are going to do, Charley. Is it something dreadful?"

"You won't tell, will you?"

"Oh, no!" they both declared.

"Well, you know how very particular he is about his front-door. I do believe he has it painted every six weeks, — at any rate, it is just as white as snow, — and I mean to go down to the store — " Here Charley shook his head eagerly, and laughed with a joyful giggle. "I mean to go to the store and buy some bright-red paint, and paint his door for him to-night, after dark."

Flora and Nelly fairly screamed with ecstasy at this delightful bit of mischief, and in an instant all three heads were close together, settling the very best way to carry it out. Flora proposed to run in and beg the cook for a small tin kettle to put the paint in. Nelly offered·to go with her to help beg, if the cook should happen to be cross; while Charley remembered that there were some old paint-brushes in the garret, and he would hunt them up; then they would all go to the store to choose the paint, and after dark they would steal softly out and take turns in painting the door.

Nelly had permission to stay at Woodlawn until nine o'clock; and as Squire Dusenberry made all his family go to bed as soon as it was dark, and was snoring himself by half-past eight, they had not the slightest fear of being discovered.

"We'll make the most dreadful bogy on the door that ever was seen, — won't we?" said Charley, jumping on and off his seat with glee at the thought; "we'll give him seven rows of teeth and ten horns."

"And all the people going to church to-morrow will be so frightened they will jump half over the moon," cried Nelly, laughing and clapping her hands.

"Just fancy Squire Dusenberry," said Flora; " this is the way he will look at it ; " and she opened her eyes till they seemed ready to pop out, and stretched her mouth very nearly from ear to ear ; and then all three laughed and jumped and wished .it was dark, so that they might begin painting the bogy right away.

Oh, oh! what naughty children ! Squire Dusenberry had done wrong, certainly, but two wrongs never did make a right, and never will.

Nelly by this time had quite forgotten her good resolutions, and waited impatiently with the other two. They could hardly eat enough tea, they were in such a hurry, and ran all the way to the little store in the village, where for ten cents Charley got the old tin mug the cook had given them, half full of such bright-red paint that one look at it would have made a bull as mad as forty Indians.

Soon after the sun set behind the hills, the gorgeous red and purple faded out of the clouds, and Madam Twilight softly laid her gray mantle upon the earth. Mr. Rivers sat with his wife in the cosy little porch at the back of the parsonage, admiring the peaceful scene, and talking lovingly about Nelly, — how good she had been lately, and how she had made herself so dear, so dear to their hearts.

Where was Nelly at this moment? One of three little crouching figures before what had been Squire Dusenberry's clean white door, trembling, half-repentant, watching, while Charley, brush in hand, was daubing the sides with streaks of red paint, criss-cross, up and down, here and there, in every direction ; while in the middle the dreadful bogy, something like this,* had already been painted, — looking perfectly fearful, with its staring eyes and many horns, seen in the dim light of the stars.

" There ! " whispered Charley, as he put the last streak on, and turned up his tin cup quite

* Look at the opposite page.

empty, — "there! that's elegant! Walk up,
ladies and gentlemen, and you will see Squire

Dusenberry with six horns on his head, and all
the rest eyes and ears. Nothing to pay. Walk
up!"

But the girls did not walk up, — they ran
away; for now that the mischief was done,
they began to be both frightened and sorry;

and when they got back to Woodlawn, Nelly
was glad that it was nine o'clock, and hastened
home, with Sam the stable-boy to escort her,
ashamed to meet the eye of Flora's mother.

Once at home, she did not run as usual to
sit upon her kind father's knee, and tell him
and her mother all she had seen and done.
No. Guilty conscience, looking exactly like
the bogy on the Squire's door, seemed staring
her in the face from all the doors in the parsonage, and she hurried up to her own little
room.

Undressing herself as quickly as she could,
and gabbling over her prayers in a nervous,
frightened way, she jumped into bed.

Ah! I fear she had lost some of her "great
riches."

"I wonder what can be the matter with
Nelly," said Mrs. Rivers down-stairs to her
husband. "She must have tired herself out
with play."

" I hope she has done nothing wrong at Woodlawn," said Mr. Rivers.

" Oh, dear, no! She is so happy there that she behaves beautifully. Poor little darling! she is only tired," answered the loving mother.

CHAPTER VII.

DISCOVERY.

THE sun rose the next morning bright and hot, and long before the church-bells began to ring it had dried up the dew, and shone with a quivering melting glare all over the land, and 'way out to the wide shining sea, where the ships lay like little white specks on its bosom.

It shone just as bright and hot on Squire Dusenberry's front-door, and baked the dreadful bogy there hard and fast. As it was Sunday, no one passed the house before church-time. Squire Dusenberry and his family always went out of the house, Sundays and every other day, by the back-door, so as to leave no footmarks on the steps. If any one chanced to visit them, the very instant they left, one of the Squire's daughters came out to sweep and dust the steps after them, and polish the finger-marks off of the brass knocker.

The Squire went stumping about in his vegetable garden before breakfast, with his hands under his coat-tails, and saying to himself, " Oh, dear me ! just look at my cabbages ! just look at my cabbages ! " and he was n't a bit sorry for killing the poor rabbits.

Then the breakfast-bell rang, and he stumped back into the house, sat down at the table, took his hands from beneath his coat-tails, mumbled out a grace in a very disrespectful manner, ate two pork-chops, three baked potatoes, four slices of bread, and drank a great cup of coffee, — enough breakfast for one man, *I* should think, and a little over.

But all these good things did not make him an atom better-tempered, for he kicked the dog the moment he got up from the table, scolded his wife, boxed his daughter's ears for not finding his pipe in half a quarter of a minute, and

sat down in a corner to smoke and twiddle his
thumbs one over the other, until it was time to
go to church. As to reading the Bible or
some good book, he never thought of such a
thing.

Ding-dong! Ding-dong! Ding-dong!

The people began to move along the wide
pleasant village street on their way to church.
Stout old farmers, with white hair, but still
hale and strong, their good old wives hanging
on their arms, and half a dozen children follow-
ing on behind, passed up the quiet street; wag-
ons and carriages, bringing their owners from a
distance, rattled past; and one and all stared in
astonishment at Squire Dusenberry's door, and
thought he must certainly have gone raving
mad. But the old Squire and his family saw
nothing. As I have told you, they came out
of the house by the back-door, and never looked
behind them when they walked round to the
front gate.

Everybody watched him in church. They
saw him take his old iron spectacles out of his
pocket, find the hymn, and tune up through his
nose, 'way behind the red-headed chorister, just
the same as ever. Charley, Flora, and Nelly
were perhaps more astonished than the rest, for
they could not understand why he took the mischief so quietly. As to the good minister and
Mrs. Rivers, they had not seen the door, for
they always looked straight before them when
they went to church, with their thoughts on
things not of this world.

But when the service was over, and the people, as usual in country places, greeted each
other standing outside around the church-porch,
an old deacon said to the Squire, —

" Glad to see you taking it so easy."

" Taking what so easy ? " growled the other.

" Why, the scandalous red picter on your
front-door, for I don't 'spose you did it."

" What ? ! ! red picture ? Are you perform-
ing on a long bow for my benefit ? "

The Squire meant by that, that he thought
the Deacon was telling a lie.

" I don't shoot long bows," said the Deacon,
" specially on Sunday.   I saw a great red goblin painted on your door, and I thought you
knew all about it."

" I saw it too, — an awful critter ! " said a
weazen-faced old farmer, who was whittling a
small chip.

" So did I," cried a fat old lady, busy eating
a large slice of gingerbread.

I wish you could have seen Squire Dusenberry then !   He started out of the churchyard
at a pace as if he meant to beat the railroad, as
the man always does who carries the President's
message.   His wife and daughters tried to
keep up with him, but without success, for the
old Squire had got into his gate, and was already dancing up and down with rage, in a way
to crack the very flagstones, before the dreadful
bogy which was staring at him from his door.

He had been thus dancing five minutes before his family got there, and that was very lucky for them.

"Who did it? who did it?" he screamed. "I'll have them put in prison! I'll beat them to powder!"

He was still dancing and screaming in this way, — bad enough, goodness knows, for weekdays, but oh! how dreadful on the Sabbath, — when the good minister came along, with Mrs. Rivers, and Nelly holding fast to her father's hand.

Surprised at such unusual sounds, Mr. Rivers and his wife looked up, — and then they saw the frightful door, — at the same moment that Nelly gave a violent start.

"I'll have them tarred and feathered! I'll duck them in the horse-pond!" cried Squire Dusenberry; at which awful threats Nelly turned ghastly white, and so giddy, that it seemed as if the trees and houses and church-steeple were all bobbing around; but it was she who was staggering and reeling, as if she had suddenly become tipsy.

"Why, Nelly, my child, are you ill? What is the matter?" said her father, taking her up in his arms.

"Oh, papa!" she gasped, with white and trembling lips, "don't let him do it, — take me home with you; oh! don't let him touch me!"

A miserable unhappy suspicion darted into both parents' minds, as they listened to Nelly's entreaty. They quickened their steps and were soon safe within the parsonage.

"Oh!" cried Nelly, bursting into tears, "how pleasant this room looks! I don't want ever to leave it."

It was the very same room of which she had been so tired, and her parents were still more surprised to hear her say this.

"Nelly, my little daughter, tell me, — have

you been doing anything wrong? Do you know who painted the Squire's door?" asked her father, in a sad, kind tone.

The blood rushed in great tides over the child's face and neck. She had never told a lie since she knew how very wicked it was. She could not tell one now. Oh, no! Nelly would have SCORNED to utter a lie.

And so, after a great struggle, her quivering lips opened, and the words "I helped" came like a great sob from them.

And then, with many tears, the whole story came out, about the rabbits and the children's anger, and the revenge they took; and the kind loving reproof and teachings of her father made the little girl feel more and more sorry that she had returned evil for evil, and was farther away than ever from that "godliness" which is "great riches." Grieving and re-pentant, she was quite ready to promise that she would go with her father and beg Squire

Dusenberry to forgive her share in the mischief which had enraged him so.

But more than this, — when she went to bed that night, Nelly prayed from her inmost heart to become a better child, and said with a new and solemn reverence this beautiful prayer in verse : —

"Make me, O Lord! a sinless child,
As Christ was pure and undefiled.
Help me to come to Thee each day,
As Christ has bidden us, to pray.
May I forbear to seek my own,
For Christ has said, — ' *Thy* will be done.'
And to myself prefer my brother,
For Christ has said, — ' Love one another.'
Give my dear mother honor fit,
As Christ to Mary did submit.
Be ever candid in my youth,
For Christ commandeth, — ' Love the truth.'
May I to others e'er be mild,
As Christ was silent when reviled.
And still with meekness bear my part,
For Christ has blessed ' the poor in heart.'
And when upon my dying bed,
May Christ's dear arms be round my head.

There, folded on the gentle breast
Of Christ, I 'll find my perfect rest."

The next morning, immediately after breakfast, Nelly went with her father to Woodlawn,
where he had a very serious conversation with
the kind parents of Flora and Charley. All
three felt that the Squire had been very cruel
in killing the poor rabbits, and really deserved
some punishment, though not the one he got.

Flora and Charley were very willing to say
they were sorry. So they all marched over, the
three little penitents, begging Mr. Rivers and
Mr. Gray to go first and break the dreadful
news.

It did not make them feel any more comfortable when they saw a man scraping away
for dear life, trying to get the red goblin off the
door, and I am sorry to tell that Squire Dusenberry did not receive their apologies in the
very best spirit. " Fiddlesticks and nonsense! "
he jerked out; " keep your rabbits to yourself

next time.   You've got to pay for daubing up my door!   So you see you have advanced three steps backwards in your fun, for it will take the whole of your pocket-money for the next three months ; and all the *tarts* you buy will be very sour *goose*berry tarts."

CHAPTER VIII.

TRY, TRY AGAIN.

FOR several weeks after the dreadful affair
of the bogy on Squire Dusenberry's door, Nelly
was just as good as it is possible for a human
being to be in this world, — and that is by no
means perfect. We shall all be able to travel
down *through* the world to China, instead of
going all the way round it, before we find abso-
lute perfection in any one, big or little. And
as it is not at all probable that this will take
place in our day, we 'll give up looking for
perfection, like sensible people, and go on with
the story.

So Nelly took care of the baby, and helped
her mother make doughnuts, and learned her
lessons and said her prayers all these weeks,
with not above a dozen cross faces coming

down over her own, which I consider remarkable. Her father thought it remarkable too, and one evening, to reward her, he wrote something on his best sermon-paper and handed it to her, saying, — " Here, Nelly ; this is to be read to you to-morrow."

" Did you write it on purpose for me, papa ? " she asked, in a joyful tone.

" Yes," he said.

" Is it a little sermon ? "

" Yes, a week-day one, — such a sermon as ought to be preached to ·children, for it is a story with a ·moral ; and I want *you* to make the application, my darling."

" How ' application,' papa ? "

" Why, after you have read the story, I want you to tell me what lesson it teaches to you, and that is making an application."

" Oh, yes, I will, papa," the little girl replied, with an affectionate kiss ; and off she ran to bed, for it was time to go.

The next morning after breakfast, Nelly
called Willie and Maity, who sat down with
their thumbs in their mouths, so as to be sure
not to interrupt or lose a single word; and
taking up a pillow-case which she was over-
handing, cried, " Now, mamma, we 'll be the
congregation and you shall be the minister, for
papa said this was a sermon for children; and
it 's a story too.   Come, baby Bessie is fast
asleep; please begin, .dear mamma."

So Mrs. Rivers took the paper and read as
follows : —

CHAPTER IX.

OVER A BRIDGE.

A FAIRY TALE OF HOME.

In the snuggest of little toll-houses, in the centre of a long bridge, its cosy doorway nestling beneath the shadow of the sloping roof, there once lived an old toll-gatherer named Job Hapgood.

The toll-house was the merest baby-house of a place, with only three tiny rooms within, but then they fairly shone all over with the constant scrubbings and rubbings of Trot Hapgood, Job's only daughter, who was the neatest and nicest little body you can imagine.

The walls of the sitting-room were half covered with staring red and blue posters, setting forth the glories of various travelling-shows, mingled with advertising pictures, in which people were represented in the act of dyeing

their clothes the color of indigo with " Huzzard's Blueing," or looking with amazement at
their faces reflected in their own shoes, polished
with " Buzzard's Blacking "; but, after all, this
was rather ornamental than otherwise, and if
Job Hapgood had been a good-natured man,
they might have amused him very much.

But, you see, he was not good-natured.   He
did nothing but grumble because he was obliged
to put them up, and would have liked to make
Huzzard swallow all Buzzard's blacking, and
painted up Buzzard like an ancient Briton with
all Huzzard's blueing, and so got rid of both
out of hand.

Well, one bright summer's day, just as the
clock struck twelve, old Job Hapgood popped
his grizzled head out of the little sentry-box on
one side of the door, where he stood to take
tolls, and sniffing something like cooking in
the air, concluded it must be about his dinner-
time.   So he shuffled into the house, with his

nose all wrinkled up in a discontented sort of way, plainly taking it for granted that there was nothing particular for dinner, and it was just his luck.

"Ah, there *you* are, father!" cried Trot's cheery voice; "and here's your dinner, all piping hot."

"Yes, yes, my dear," replied Job, shuffling off to one side, to pretend he did n't see what Trot was dishing up,—"yes, yes, I'm coming in a minute."

"Oh, no,—you must come now!" said Trot, merrily. "Just take your seat,—that's a dear old daddy,—and see what I've got for you! First, here's a nice dish of boiled beef and potatoes; and *there* you are,"—setting down the first dish; "and your tea drawn just the way you like it; and *there* you are again,"—setting down a small brown tea-pot; "and for a treat, a delicious little bit of—what do you think?" asked Trot, mysteriously, clasping her hands.

" I 'm sure I don't know," said Job, disconsolately. " *Anything* 's good enough for *me*."

" Tripe ! " cried Trot, fairly clapping her hands in joyous triumph. " I bought it for you myself, and stewed it down with onions ; and *there* you are ! " — and Trot set the tripe on the table, in a brown earthen bowl, and tripped round to give her father a little squeeze, and a little kiss on the very tip of his nose, — laughing all the time with a trill like a happy bird.

" Yes, yes, Trot my dear," replied the toll-gatherer, — " you 're a good little girl to your poor old daddy. I don't know what would become of me without you ; " and his eye rested on the staring placards of Huzzard's Blueing and Buzzard's Blacking with an inward discontent which even tripe could n't make him forget.

" Oh, never mind the 'tisements now, father," said Trot, cheerily ; " your dinner will be stone-cold. Come ; " and drawing her chair up to the table, she bowed her pretty golden head to ask a blessing, and the toll-gatherer was fairly settled to his dinner.

Then to see Trot hover about him, so anxious that he should be comfortable! To see her now putting a savory bit of meat on his plate, — now pouring out his tea and taking a saucy sip from the cup herself, — anon running to the door to receive a toll, then back again, singing like some blithe little bird; and presently cutting bread for her father, in a profound fiction that he was quite unable to help himself! Darling little Trot!

Then, when dinner was over, how she took his pipe from the mantel-shelf, and with a thousand graceful little gestures — still very like a bird — began filling it! pressing the tobacco down with her chubby forefinger in proper style, and then putting it between his lips to be lighted, with an approving pat on his brown cheek, and setting the cricket under his feet for him to take his afternoon nap, before

she tripped away to clear the table. Busy
little Trot!

Now, surely, if never before, Job Hapgood
ought to have felt contented with his lot, as he
sat in his arm-chair smoking and looking ab-
sently about the room. And yet he *was* thinking, not of the blessings he enjoyed, but how
many years he had been toll-gatherer on that
bridge, and after all, what a poor, mean,
scraping, toiling kind of life it was for an old
man. Gradually these thoughts became mixed
up with his dislike for the showbills, and he
was just beginning to feel rather drowsy, and
a little confused as to whether Huzzard's Blueing was the Grand Calithumpian Moral Egyp-
tian Caravan, or Buzzard's Blacking was the
Real, Living Jackass with Four Tails, or both
together, when suddenly he was aroused by
some one's calling him from without. The
voice was rather an odd one too, — high and
shrill, like the whistling of the wind through a

keyhole, and, moreover, whoever was calling seemed to be in the greatest possible hurry to pay their toll and be off again.

" Coming ! " shouted Job, sleepily ; and rousing himself as well as he could, he hurried to the door, and there he saw a very curious-looking vehicle indeed.

There certainly was something out of the way about this conveyance ! It was n't a travelling-coach, or a top-buggy, or an Adams's Express, or a steam-mower ; it bore not the slightest resemblance to a tilbury, a dog-cart, a phaeton, a trotting-wagon, or a hearse ; it did n't look like a caravan, and nobody would have suspected it of being a perambulator ; yet it seemed to be made up with little bits out of each and all these vehicles. Harnessed to it were four spirited horses, which plunged and reared, and all but stood on their tails with impatience ; but neither driver nor passenger could be seen anywhere.

Job stood staring with all his eyes at this queer affair, when once more the voice from within exclaimed, " Come here, and take your toll, Job Hapgood."

Half-scared out of his wits, yet compelled, as it seemed, by some spell, the toll-gatherer went up to the strange conveyance and laid his hand on the knob of the door.

The instant he did so, the door flew open of itself; he was whisked into the carriage, he could not tell how, and, like a flash, off they went down the road, pell-mell, helter-skelter !

" Oh, good land ! " yelled Job Hapgood at the top of his lungs. " Oh, my goodness ! For pity's sake ! Help ! Murder ! Fire ! Oh, Trot, Trot, Trot ! "

But of what use was it to shout and bawl in an enchanted coach ? for such this must certainly have been. Moreover, the toll-gatherer's voice seemed to sink into a whisper, like a person's in a nightmare, and his tongue to become glued to his palate with fear, when on looking round him he found himself — ALONE.

Yes, there he sat, — alone with the Voice which had summoned him from his home, — no shadowy form, no gauzy garment hovering at his side, yet he felt that invisible eyes were piercing to his very soul. A cold chill crept over his limbs, his hair rose on end, and in the extremity of terror his teeth chattered in his head.

Suddenly the silence was broken by a mocking laugh close at his ear.

" Oh, my heart alive, what's that? " gasped Job.

" Why, Job, my fine fellow! " said the Voice, " you don't seem grateful for your good luck! Ten minutes ago you were a miserable man, disgusted with your lot in life; yet now you find yourself in a splendid carriage, rolling straight towards happiness, and all you say is, 'Help!' and 'Murder!' Ha, ha, ha! "

"B—but who—but what—" stammered the toll-gatherer.

"Who is with you? A friend of yours, Job,—one who is going to put you in a new situation," returned the Voice, with mock gravity.

"But please your—your—dreadful majesty," faltered Job, who really began to think he had fallen into the hands of somebody he called Old Gooseberry,—"I want my daughter Trot with me, wherever I am."

"Well, it's you for making conditions!" retorted his unseen companion. "Suppose you sit still and only speak when you're spoken to!" and with that down came a sounding whack on Job Hapgood's head, which made darkness, besprinkled with a curious pattern of stars, swim before his eyes, and advised him pretty strongly to say nothing more, but wait and see what would happen next.

All at once, plump! they pulled up, and stood stock-still. The door flew open, Job was impelled, as before, to get out, and in an instant strange carriage, fast horses, and all disappeared in a flash of lightning, and left him alone once more with the Voice.

The place where he now found himself was a long bridge, spanning a rapid river, whose dark waters flowed with a murmuring sound among the massive beams and abutments below, until they fell, with a subdued, yet ceaseless roar, over vast masses of jagged rocks, cutting the waters into myriad wreaths of foam and spray. The sun shed a dreary and awful light through the thick dun-colored mist which completely shrouded either shore, and the whole scene oppressed and weighed upon the soul like the heavy shadow of some dreadful dream.

In the centre of the bridge one familiar object appeared, — a toll-house, whose weather-beaten walls and sloping roof reminded Job very much of his own home, — once so despised, though now he would have given anything on earth to get back again.

"Well, there's a toll-house, at any rate," he thought ; "it must be a common bridge, after all."

"Oh no, it is not, Job," said the Voice, — which seemed to know his inmost idea, — "it is the site of all your happiness."

"What! am I to be a toll-gatherer again?" cried Job, — that is, he thought he cried, for in reality his voice was the lowest whisper. "No, thank you. If that's the best luck you've got for me, why let's go back to the old place."

"Not just yet, Job," returned the Voice. "You have a lesson of happiness to learn first."

"Oh, of course. I'm bound to be contented and happy with toiling and moiling from morning till night, and night till morning, — and one's very sitting-room invaded with 'tisements! — which, if I could have the fixin' of things, I'd Huzzard and Buzzard 'em, — a pack of four-tailed jackasses! At my age, too, — rising sixty! If you could make me young again, that would be something like happiness. There were good times then, — ah, dear, dear!" Here his tirade was interrupted by the Voice.

"Look, Job," it said, — and its tones were deep and solemn now as the murmur of many waters, — "something is passing over the bridge."

The slow rumbling of a heavy wagon sounded in the distance, and in a moment more it emerged from the mist on the left bank of the river, and the timbers of the bridge resounded under the tread of two strong farm-horses.

A sturdy fellow walked beside the wagon, which was half filled with hay, making a soft nest for two merry children who rode within.

As it approached the toll-house, one of the children, a pretty fair-haired boy, sprang up, exclaiming, — "Oh, Uncle Hiram! let me pay the toll, — won't you? Look, Faith; now I'm

General Warren a-wavin' his sword at Bun-
ker Hill! Hurray!" and the child flourished
a long cornstalk as he spoke, his eyes sparkling with glee.

"Do you recognize that boy, Job?" asked
the Voice.

The toll-gatherer turned ghastly pale, and
his voice had a strange, hollow sound as he
answered, —

"Myself!"

"You were happy *then*, Job?" said the
Voice.

"Very, very happy!" groaned the toll-
gatherer. The wagon stopped at the toll-house,
and the boy held out an ancient Continental
coin. Moved by a power he could not resist,
Job came forward to receive it, when the boy,
fixing his eyes upon him, uttered a terrified
cry. In an instant the wagon had passed
swiftly on, and was lost in the shadows beyond.

"My poor uncle Hiram!" sighed Job.

"He was shot at Bennington fifty years ago."

As he spoke, he looked once more towards the left bank of the river, and saw a singular change in the dark mist that overhung the shore like a funeral pall. Slowly it rolled backwards on either side; and just where it was parted, the toll-gatherer saw the distinct picture of a room in an antiquated farm-house. A dim light, burning within the wide chimney, gleamed over the time-worn furniture; a high-backed chair beside the hearth; a tester bedstead covered by a patch-work quilt; and on the wall above, a faded sampler wrought with texts from Scripture. In the centre of the room, on rough trestles, reposed a child's coffin, covered with a sheet.

"My mother's room!" exclaimed Job, the cold dew starting to his brow. "But whose coffin is that?"

As he spoke, the clouds rolled heavily back

and hid the vision from his sight. At the
same moment the awful toll of a funeral-bell
filled the air; and issuing from the dim mist,
with the sound of many horses' feet, a burial-
train passed on over the bridge. Solemnly it
moved along and stopped opposite the toll-
house. Suddenly the side of the hearse became transparent, and the child's coffin was
revealed within — the lid partly drawn aside.
The toll-gatherer moved closer, and fixed his
terrified eyes upon the marble face of the
corpse.

"Whose funeral is this, Job?" asked the
Voice.

"My little sister's!" sobbed the toll-gatherer.

Like the swift passage of a dream the burial-
train passed onwards, amid the doleful clangor
of the bells, and vanished in the gloom.

"Then there were sorrows clouding your
early youth?" asked the Voice.

"She was the darling of the house!" cried

the poor toll-gatherer. " Oh, Ruth, dear little Ruth!"

" The clouds are parting again," continued the Voice. " See what they bear on their dark bosoms!"

Within the framework of the first shadowy picture appeared another vision. It showed the outside of the same farm-house, surrounded by an old-fashioned garden. Fruit-trees drooped their loaded branches over the wide beds where flowers and sweet-herbs grew together. The porch in front of the door was faintly lighted by the new moon, and there sat a handsome young man and woman.

You could see in their happy faces a strong likeness to the children who rode so merrily in the hay-cart long ago, and from the way her dark glossy curls rested against his breast it seemed as though they were newly married.

" Who are these happy ones, Job?" questioned the Voice.

" Me and Faith Trueman," murmured Job.
" We were just married then, and living as
happy as a pair of little birds. We had our
bit of money laid up against a rainy day, and
everything nice around us. Oh dear ! oh dear !
A hard thing for a man to come to poverty
at last when all began so well."

The vision passed away as he spoke. It
seemed to carry with it some of the uncertain
light that before shone over bridge and river, or
else the day was really drawing to a close, when,
plodding wearily from the hidden shore, two
wayfarers appeared on the hither end of the
bridge. The principal figure was a man in the
prime of life, but sadly worn and haggard as
though with many troubles. He supported on
his arm a woman, whose dark hood, pushed
back from her face, revealed her pale beautiful
features and raven hair. Each of them carried
a bundle, which seemed to contain all their
worldly possessions, and the dust of the weary
road hung heavily upon their garments.

As they passed the toll-house they turned their heads, and looked Job Hapgood full in the face.

A deadly chill seemed to strike into his very heart; he shuddered from head to foot: for in these wayworn figures he recognized himself and his wife.

" You suffered like this in your manhood?" said the Voice, with strange gentleness in its tones.

" There was one hard season after another," cried Job, clasping his thin hands in bitter grief. " My crops failed more than any of the neighbors'; and though I strove and struggled against poverty and sickness, there came debt upon debt, and at last the very homestead went from us. Ah, Faith! poor birdie! That I should have brought thee to this! Cruel! cruel!"

" Look, Job!" broke in the Voice, — " see what figure this is that passes over the bridge!"

The daylight had faded away, and a gloomy nightfall settled blackly down on the river. As the thick clouds drifted sullenly apart, the dim, watery light of the moon streamed between them, and fell on the form of a man hastening over the bridge. His clothes hung in tatters round his wasted form, and his long, tangled hair and beard mingled in wild confusion about a wan face which still bore some shadowy likeness to the fair boy of years ago.

He paused as he reached the centre of the bridge, where a wooden seat was placed for poor wayfarers, and placing gently upon it a sort of bundle that he carried in his arms, wrapped in an old shawl, he stood gazing downwards at the rushing water.

"This is the place," he said at last, in hoarse and broken tones. "Here, where we toiled along, heart-broken, from our happy home, — where I saw the light fade out of my darling's eyes, and did not die! I, who had brought her to such a pass! Here I have come at last, to join her! Trot, little birdie, oh, farewell forever!" and his voice choked with sobs, his desperate hands clenched above his head, — the wretched man hovered one instant over eternity ——

"Stop!" rang out a voice, loud and commanding, as the tall form of a man darted towards the suicide, and clasped him firmly in his arms. "For heaven's sake! — what would you do?"

"Ah, let me die!" cried the figure, cowering and grovelling under the strong grasp. "What have I to live for but starvation and despair?"

The other pushed him down on the bench, and taking the seeming bundle in his arms, drew aside the old shawl. The fair face of a sleeping infant appeared, the moonbeams falling like a glory on its little golden head.

"My child!" cried Job Hapgood, falling on his knees. "My little darling, innocent child!"

The shadows fell deeper and darker on the bridge as the toll-gatherer, lifting his head from his clasped hands, raised his eyes towards the Voice.

" You do not condemn me utterly ? " he humbly entreated. " I was mad — lost — I know not what, under my heavy load of troubles. He pitied me even in my wickedness, although he was a man of God " ——

" And took you and the child to his home, feeding and sheltering you there, until, through his unwearied kindness " ——

" I got the place as toll-gatherer ! " cried Job ; " and, please GOD, I 'll pray for and bless him many a long year to come."

" Look at the shadows once more, Job," said the Voice. " See what they show you now."

Job looked toward the shore, and there, limned forth on the dark background of the mist, he beheld his little sitting-room at home. The blazing fire shed a rosy light upon the whitewashed walls, gay with the familiar

signs of Huzzard and Buzzard, which the cheerful gleam transformed into charming pictures;
while the bright tins on the mantel glittered like
homely diamonds.   In the centre of the room
stood the tea-table, spread with its clean brown
cloth and well-known sprigged china ; no sound
could be heard but the busy tick of the Dutch
clock and the singing of the kettle on the fire ;
and close beside the hearth, her sweet face illu-
mined with a tender blush, as the firelight played
on it, sat Trot at her sewing.

" Oh, Trot, dear, darling little Trot! " cried
Job Hapgood, springing to his feet. " If I
only can get back to you again, I 'll be the most
contented man in the State of Vermont! "

" What! with Huzzard, Buzzard, and all ? "
inquired the Voice, which had recovered somewhat of its former sarcastic tone.

" With every one of 'em ! " shouted Job at
the top of his voice, giving a frantic flourish
with his feet, half-joy, half-impatience, which
kicked over —

The Voice?

No, the cricket. . . . . "Why, bless me, father!" cried Trot, running up to him, "what's come over you? Have n't you had a good nap?"

"Nap! my birdie," exclaimed Job, staring at her in amazement; "have I been *asleep?*"

"Yes! the best part of an hour, and snoring away with your dear old mouth as wide open as the drawbridge."

Job paused for a moment to give Trot a delighted hug and kiss, to make sure he had really got her all safe; then raising her face by the round, dimpled chin, so as to look in her eyes, he said, —

"Tell me, birdie, do you love the old house?"

"Why, surely, father," said Trot, looking in his face with a wondering smile.

"And you'd rather have it, 'tisements and all, than any other in the world?"

"To be sure I would!" said Trot, earnestly.

" Why, have n't we lived here winter and summer for fifteen years ? Don't we know and love the breeze, and the river, and the old bridge, as well as if they were our own ? And could we be as happy anywhere else as we are here, — where the dear memories of the years that are past hang round the walls to make them beautiful and holy, father ? "

" Why then, I 'll tell you what, Trot ! " cried Job, gathering her little figure closely in his arms, and laying his brown cheek tenderly on her pretty head, — " I 'd not change it for a king's palace anywheres ! I 'll love it henceforth for your sake, my birdie ; and as to Huzzard and Buzzard — why, bless their hearts ! " cried Job, lifting his glowing face and looking round the room, — " if any one was to tell me I did n't look upon those men as brothers, I 'd wish they might never see a four-tailed jackass as long as they lived ! So give me a kiss, Trot ! "

And so she did.

"Oh, what a beautiful, beautiful story!" said Nelly, with a sigh of pleasure, as her mother finished.

"And have you made the application?" asked Mrs. Rivers, gently.

"Is it that I, also, must be grateful and contented?" asked the little girl, in a low voice.

"Yes; and if you are truly contented and grateful, if you bear without murmuring all the trials of this life, you will surely win a portion of that godliness which will entitle you to a home in heaven. And you will also be far happier here, my little Nelly. God will bless you here; never doubt it."

For several weeks after this, Nelly was grateful and contented, though not without many a rebellious and envious twinge in her heart; but she fought every one of them down; and her kind parents encouraged her and loved her, oh, so dearly! so dearly! that her search after godliness was made far more simple and easy for her than for many another little pilgrim on this earth, whose path was filled with the sharp stumbling-blocks of temptation, poverty, and neglect.

It was now late in October. The dry leaves rustled in the paths; the little birds were flying every day to the warm southern lands; and fires looked cheery and pleasant.

The Grays had gone to the great city of New York — to their winter home; and Nelly's rosy face had oftentimes a melancholy expression, for she sadly missed her dear playmates, Flora and Charley.

One day a letter came to the parsonage, which caused deep anxiety. It was from Mrs. Gray, and contained an invitation for Nelly to spend the winter with her friends. Mrs. Gray promised to care for and watch over both the little girls alike; and she wished that Nelly should take lessons with Flora in music, French, and drawing. She begged to have her until spring, and as much longer as her parents could spare her.

"Oh, mamma! papa! do, — *do* let me go!" cried Nelly, her eyes sparkling, her face glowing with eagerness. "Oh, I want to go so much!"

"Will my little Nelly come home as happy and contented as she seems to be now?" asked her father, in a gentle tone.

"Oh, yes, yes!" she answered. "I don't care a bit about fine things now, — that is, not near so much as I *did*," added the truthful child; "and I *will* strive and fight harder than ever to be contented and grateful, — but oh, papa! I want to learn music and drawing. Only think! I shall know how to draw the parsonage, and the grand old elm-tree opposite, if I practise ever so much; and perhaps I can take your likeness," — and she ran up to her father, and, curling her arms round his neck, said, — "Do let me go!" with her lips tight pressed against his cheek.

With many prayers and some misgivings, permission was at last given, and a few days after, the little trunk was packed, and Nelly went to bed an hour earlier the previous evening, to make the next morning nearer.

The first sunbeam that darted into the room woke her up, and, all in a tremble for joy that the happy day was come, Nelly dressed herself, said her prayers in a hurry, and ran down-stairs to breakfast.

" Good-morning, papa! good-morning, mamma! " she said. " I never felt so happy in my whole life. It will be so good for my health to go travelling."

" Is your health very delicate ? " asked Mr. Rivers, laughing.

" Oh dear, no, papa! I have n't an ache or a pain in so much as the ends of my hair, but then you know it is so perfectly delightful to travel. Oh, I could jump over the house for joy ! "

Nelly could scarcely eat, she was so excited. She had given her box of ninepins to Willie and Maity, and her cry-baby doll to little Bessie ; — so her little brothers kissed her for good-bye, all smiles and delight in their new present ; and little Bessie was too busy holding the cry-baby upsidedown and shaking it, to notice her at all ; — but a few great tears came into Nelly's eyes as her kind mother folded her close to her heart, and prayed the good God to bless and keep her darling, and shield her from all harm to soul and body.

VOL. III.   10

CHAPTER X.

NELLY IN NEW YORK.

THE Grays had moved this autumn into an elegant mansion on Fifth Avenue. As the carriage containing Mr. Rivers and Nelly drove up to the door, and they alighted and went up the high flight of steps, the little girl's heart beat wildly, and for the first time she felt as if she did not want her father to leave her.

"Does Mrs. Gray live here?" inquired Mr. Rivers of the dandified-looking black waiter.

"Mrs. Gray *resides* here," answered the man in a reproving tone, and with a contemptuous glance at the plainly-dressed little girl.

They entered the wide hall paved with marble, and then the waiter said, —

"Will you give me your card, sir?"

"I have no card," answered the good clergyman, simply. "Tell her that Mr. Rivers and his daughter have come."

Then they went into the splendid parlor, and Nelly stood like one entranced. I do not care to waste ink and paper on a description of furniture, — half of the wicked, silly novels which are written are made up of such descriptions. I will only say that, to the child's wondering eyes and thoughts, all that was not blazing with gold seemed to be velvet and satin; the little plain parsonage parlor faded almost out of her memory; and when Flora flew down the long stairs and into the room, and caught Nelly in her arms, kissing her over and over, not the faintest longing for her home was left.

Mr. Rivers stayed, an honored and welcome guest, until the next day, and then bade his little daughter good-bye. His last words were whispered in her ear; they were, — "Remember, Nelly, that 'Godliness is great riches.'"

CHAPTER XI.

TEMPTATION.

" DEAR me! I wish I could wear corsets," said Nelly, the second morning of her visit. She was looking on with admiring eyes as Flora, with her hands on her hips, holding in her breath, was being laced up by her maid.

" I 've only just begun to wear them myself," said Flora. " They don't feel so very comfortable, but mamma says I am getting so crooked."

" And what a splendid big hoop-skirt you have got ; and, I declare! you are going to put on a flounced dress ! "

" Well, what of that ? " inquired Flora. " I like your brown merino without flounces just as well. If you like, I will beg mamma to give you some corsets and flounced dresses too."

"Oh, thank you!" cried Nelly. "I should like them of all things; I would be laced up *so* tight, and have the dearest little waist! and I do *love* flounces."

The petition was made and willingly granted. Mrs. Gray never imagined that she could harm her little guest by dressing her in fine clothes; and before the week was out, Nelly and Flora went to take a walk in Madison Park, dressed like sisters, with round hats trimmed with black velvet, and bright cherry pompons, and silk dresses of a beautiful golden-brown shade, the skirt of each adorned with three little fluted flounces, headed with black velvet.

How Nelly did prink! She was laced so tight that she could scarcely breathe, and her new gaiter-boots pinched her toes dreadfully; but what of that? she was as fine and fashionable-looking as the best; and she walked along with a mincing step, glancing with disdain at some plainly dressed children who were sitting on the grass playing with the dried leaves, which had fallen from the trees.

Presently a poor, barefooted, bareheaded, little girl approached Nelly and Flora. Clasping her hands together, she whined out, " Please give me a penny, — I 've had nothing to eat to-day."

It was very likely the child was telling an untruth, for many of these city beggars are taught by their wicked, drunken parents to lie in this way; but Nelly did not know it, and if she did, she should at least have answered her kindly. But, alas! godliness had fled from her heart. She swept past, saying, in a cross tone, — " Take care ! do not come so near my dress. Go away ! "

" You 're a stuck - up Miss Proudy," returned the beggar, her eyes flashing with anger and hatred. Then calling a dirty little dog who was loitering by, — " Here, Snap, — here ! "

she cried, pointing to Nelly. "Sic 'em! sic 'em!"

In an instant the dog had bounded up to the shrieking girl, and had caught her flounced dress in his sharp teeth, while the beggar, with a mocking laugh, darted away to escape a policeman who was hurrying towards the spot.

"Oh, oh, oh!" screamed Nelly, in an agony, "take him away! take him away!" While Flora, afraid to go near, was screaming just as loudly at a little distance, wringing her hands and begging that somebody would kill the dog.

The policeman beat him off with his club, and Nelly, bursting into hysterical tears, would have fallen, if he had not caught her in his arms. Through all her tears came a dim impression that she had half deserved her terrible fright, — that she had not observed the "golden rule." When the poor little beggar had asked for a penny, she had harshly wounded the child's feelings, who in setting the dog upon

her was only revenging herself, just as Nelly,
Flora, and Charley had done when they painted
the red bogy on Squire Dusenberry's white
door.

But I am afraid even this lesson did not
reach the right spot in Nelly's heart, for
every succeeding day she seemed fonder of
dress and display, and the sweet, modest expression of her face gave way to vain and
proud looks.

It was now quite winter-time. One clear
frosty morning, as the family in Fifth Avenue
sat eating their nice breakfast, Flora broke out
with —

"Oh, mamma, I want to have a party;
won't you let me?"

"Yes, mamma, do!" put in Charley. "I
know lots of boys, and Flo can invite the
girls — crowds of them."

"A party! how enchanting!" chimed in
Nelly.

" Well, as you all seem to be of one mind about it," answered Mrs. Gray, laughing, " you may have a party; only I hope Charley's friends won't practise gymnastics over my fine sofas and chairs."

The children bounced up from the table at this kind permission, and rushed up-stairs with such loud shouts of joy that the old cook ran out of the kitchen, thinking the house was on fire. They hunted up pens, ink, and paper, and soon had a number of invitations written and sealed up very tight, as they were of the greatest importance. Then the dandified black waiter was instructed to carry them round, and implored by Flora and Charley not to make any mistakes, — and all three watched him, standing on the front stoop, till he was out of sight.

The evening of the party came. Flora and Nelly were again dressed alike, — this time in white tarlatan and broad blue sashes. Their hair had been elegantly curled all over their heads by Mr. Isabeau the fashionable barber. They each held a large bouquet of fragrant flowers, a fan, and a pocket-handkerchief trimmed with lace. Their eyes grew wildly bright as guest after guest skipped into the room, the little girls joyously kissing Flora and Nelly, and the boys shaking hands and bowing with the greatest politeness.

Flora had had parties before, and had been used to this elegance and show all her life, so, although it was very delightful, it was somewhat a matter of course to her; but Nelly was almost delirious with the enchanting excitement, and every time she caught sight of her pretty figure and curling head in one of the long glasses, a new sparkle would flash from her eyes, and she would straighten herself up until she looked like a little statue of Vanity and Pride.

Ah! if her kind, loving parents could have

seen her now! They had permitted her to make this visit, hoping that nothing but good would result, and grateful to Mrs. Gray for procuring their little Nelly instruction in accomplishments for which they could not afford to pay. Little did they dream that their dear child was taking other and far different lessons.

As Nelly was thus standing and gazing at herself in the glass, she saw Charley eagerly running up behind her. "Come," said he, "we are going to have a grand game of 'Puss-in-the-Corner.' Come along, quick!"

"Oh dear, no!" answered Nelly, turning round; "I can't, possibly; it will tumble my dress, and shake my curls too much."

"Oh, never mind your curls! it's such a jolly game. Come!"

But Nelly still refused, and walked away with her nose up in the air, fanning herself, and thinking, "If old Aunt Betsy and the lame shoemaker could only see me now, how astonished they would be! Old Aunt Betsy would lift up her hands and eyes, and say, 'For pity's sake, who is that grand young lady? It can't be Miss Nelly!' and the lame shoemaker would exclaim, 'Heart alive! Here comes the Queen of the Fairies!'"

And she *would* have looked as lovely as the sweetest and prettiest of fairy queens, *if she had been unconscious of it herself;* but the self-satisfied, vain expression of her face would have spoiled and ruined the loveliest beauty on earth.

The evening wore on amidst music, games, and, at the last, a splendid supper. There seemed to be no end of mottoes, especially those delightful pulling ones which pop off like a torpedo; and every girl and boy, when the time came to go home, had a present of a dozen or two each to take with them, which was the very best of it, they declared, as it would make plenty of fun for the next day.

And now Nelly and Flora have said good-night, and are up in their own pleasant bedroom, " talking over " the delightful party, and repeating over and over again what a nice time they had had.

All at once Nelly exclaimed, " Dear me! why, where is my beautiful fan ?   I must have left it in the parlor."

Down she ran to find it.   Not a soul was in the room, though the gaslights were still burning.   Mr. and Mrs. Gray had gone into the dining-room, and were directing the servants to wash and put away the silver.   With a quick, questioning look on sofa and chairs, Nelly gazed round and round; not seeing the fan, she was turning to leave the parlor, when she spied its long tassel hanging from the mantelpiece.   A chair was close before the fire which was still brightly burning, and pushing this nearer, she got up on it though there was no need; she could easily have reached her fan standing on the carpet.

"I'll take a good look in the glass," she said to herself, "and see if my curls are in as tight as ever."

Up she mounted, leaned forward, placed her elbows on the mantelpiece, and gazed admiringly at herself.

"How nicely they do look!" she murmured, and she curled her finger in and out of the smooth rings of hair. "Really, I can't bear to go to bed. I had no idea a barber could make my curls look so much nicer than I could. They are lovely."

She whirled half round on the chair, admiring one side, then the other; she smiled and nodded at herself, when suddenly scream upon scream resounded through the room, and Mr. and Mrs. Gray and the servants rushing in, saw Nelly flying towards them, her tarlatan dress blazing, and tongues of flame leaping up round her head and face.

For an instant all recoiled, shrinking with

fright; then Mr. Gray seizing the hearth-rug, wound it round and round the burning child, pressing out the awful flames with frenzied haste, while the rest prayed aloud, amid groans and cries of pity and terror ; and Flora and Charley, who had hurried down at the first awful scream, shrank clinging to each other outside the door, not daring to go in, livid with fear, and sobbing bitterly.

It was all out; but for a moment Mr. Gray dreaded to remove the rug, — those convulsive struggles and agonized sounds told such a dreadful tale.

When he did take it away, the servants screamed and hid their faces, while Mrs. Gray, ghastly white, received the blackened, blistering little form in her trembling arms.   Great tears rained down her pitying face, and she groaned out, " Oh, what will her parents say ! oh, my poor, poor child ! ' God have mercy upon her ! "

Tenderly was she carried up-stairs and laid

upon her bed, while the servants were told to run for their lives and bring back doctors with them, as many and as quickly as possible.

Oh, what days and nights of anguish now ensued! What sad, almost despairing faces flitted around poor Nelly's bed! A telegram had summoned her kind parents, and for many, many days after, all thought that the child must die. Flora would come and look at her for a moment, and run sobbing out of the room; and Charley would gaze at her sunken eyes and bandaged, blistered face until his lips quivered and his chest heaved with painful sighs.

" Will she live?" asked Nelly's mother, in a trembling whisper, of the grave-looking doctor, as he stood one day feeling her pulse. The child was asleep, — the first sound quiet sleep since her dreadful misfortune.

The doctor was silent for a moment. He passed his hand lightly over Nelly's forehead; a gentle perspiration was upon it; then he felt

her pulse again, and said, " I believe she is out
of danger, madam, but she will be dreadfully
disfigured."

" Thank God ! " murmured the poor mother,
sinking slowly to her knees. The grateful tears
trickled over her pale cheeks, and she lovingly
pressed her lips on the poor little hand — oh,
so thin and scarred ! — lying on the outside of
the bed.

And now came peaceful, hopeful days. Nelly,
with penitent tears, had confessed to her mother all her pride and vanity. She had received
a loving forgiveness, and had joined in fer-
vent prayers of gratitude that her life had been
spared. After the first burst of bitter sorrow
at sight of her scarred face and neck, she had
thanked God again for His mercy and goodness, and with hearty sorrow for the miserable
faults which had brought her all.this pain, and
her friends and parents so much grief and
trouble, she had formed a solemn resolve to

lead indeed a new and better life, with the blessing and help of her Saviour.

Once more Nelly is in her humble, but comfortable home. A bitter trial awaits her at
first, for Willie and Maity don't want to kiss
her ; they dislike her seamed, rough face; and
baby Bessy screams and won't come near her.

The poor little girl's heart swelled with grief,
but she struggled to hide her tears, and held
out her hands coaxingly, as her dear, loving
mother was telling her little brothers that they
must love poor sister Nelly more than ever now.

" But she looks so ugly ! " persisted Willie,
with an obstinate little kick of his foot.

" She looks so ugly *too !* " repeated Maity
after him.

" See now, Willie," said his mother, — " see
how your bad example is followed by your
brother. If you say a naughty, unkind thing,
Maity will say it too. Shall we send poor sis-

ter Nelly away, because the dreadful fire burned her tender face and hurt her, oh! so terribly?"

" N—o," stammered Willie; and he crept slowly towards her, and held up his round, rosy cheek.

Nelly kissed it softly; then Maity came up, and the dear little fellow fairly put his arms round her poor neck, and whispered, " I 'm sorry for you," at which poor Nelly burst out crying, and hid her face in his neck, quite unable to speak.

But it was not long before the children, baby Bessie and all, quite forgot about the dreadful scars, and loved Nelly as well as ever. Old Aunt Betsy, when Nelly went to see her, did indeed say, " For pity's sake! " with hands and eyes uplifted; but the rest of her speech was, " Poor lamb! poor little lamb, how she must have suffered! Well, well, it will wean her from this world, and make her home in heaven more beautiful and glorious." And

Nelly, in her inmost heart, echoed, "Pray God that it may."

And the lame shoemaker, — did he cry out, "Heart alive! here comes the Queen of the Fairies?" Ah, no. He said, "Alackaday! what a sore trouble God has brought upon my pretty bird! but He has put an angel look in her eyes. Don't grieve, dear Miss Nelly; beauty is only skin-deep; you will be dearer now than ever to the hearts that love you."

Ah, yes! so she was, and nearer and dearer to Jesus, her Friend and Brother, whom she loved and tried to obey and serve with all her might. And when summer came again, and the Grays were back in beautiful Woodlawn, Nelly was a lovelier and *merrier* companion for them than ever, — full of play and innocent fun, — for, darling children, never believe that a long face and gloomy ways are what God enjoins or likes. Oh, no; he sent us in this world to be *happy*; and it is *only* and *always* our own sins and the sins of others which make us otherwise.

Sometimes even now Nelly will give way to ill-temper and other sinful feelings, for it is quite impossible to be perfect; but her parents hope and trust, and Nelly humbly believes, that Jesus is showing her day by day how to win that " Godliness" which is " great riches."

CHAPTER XII.

CONCLUSION.

THE story was finished. Tears were glistening in the children's eyes; and good old Mrs. Marble had pulled off her spectacles, and was polishing them up on the elbow of her black dress; something had dimmed them.

"Poor little Nelly!" said Sophie, in a low voice; "I think she was cruelly punished."

An assenting murmur broke from all the rest, — when their kind mother, opening the Bible, read these words in a solemn tone: —

"Woe unto the world because of offences! for it must needs be that offences come; but woe to that man by whom the offence cometh!

"Wherefore, if thy hand or thy foot offend thee, cut them off and cast them from thee: it is better for thee to enter into life halt or maimed, rather than having two hands or two feet, to be cast into everlasting fire.

"And if thine eye offend thee, pluck it out, and cast it from thee; it is better for thee to enter into life with one eye, rather than having two eyes to be cast into hell-fire."

The loving mother softly closed the Holy Book and said, — "Was it not far better for Nelly to suffer pain and lose her beauty in this life, rather than become more and more vain and foolish, to risk eternal misery hereafter? God knows best, ' He doeth all things well; ' and as long as Nelly lives she will thank Him for her punishment."

The children had been sitting round the table during the latter part of the reading, because it had grown dark and a lamp had been lit; but the light was put down low now that the story was ended, and all went and sat out upon the porch where the moonlight came, making soft shadows. The fire-flies glimmered in the grass and out among the trees, and a gentle whispering wind, passing over the dew-laden flowers, wafted their fragrance to the happy group.

"Look here," said Mrs. Marble, whom we all know had a tender loving heart, if she *did* wear a wig and iron spectacles, — "look here: it's a beautiful story. I like your 'Aunt Fanny'; and I'm very much *obleeged* to her; and I mean to try to be a better woman from this day out, and talk to my son Gam, so that we too may win some 'godliness'; and I hope you'll all pray for the poor old woman who " ——

Here she quite broke down, and, putting on her hat, hastily bade them all good-bye; and when she parted with her favorite Fred, two great tears dropped upon his hand.

Ah! dear little hearts out in the world, won't you also try? My eyes are blinded with wishful tears as I write. If I thought my stories did you no good whatever, it would give me sharp and bitter pain. If you form habits of goodness now, you will hardly fail, with God's help, to grow up good men and women; and that you may do so, is the constant prayer of your loving

Aunt Fanny.

END OF VOL. III.

CPSIA information can be obtained
at www.ICGtesting.com
Printed in the USA
BVHW030912221121
622224BV00001B/7